FUNDRAISING ROCKET

HOW ANYBODY CAN RAISE MONEY FOR ANYTHING

CASEY GRAHAM

FUNDRAISING ROCKET
Published by Casey Graham and The Rocket Company
PO Box 1918
Cumming, GA 30028 U.S.A.
The Rocket Company logo is a registered trademark of The Rocket Company, LLC.

All rights reserved. No part of this book may be reproduced or used in any form without written permission from the publisher.

Visit www.therocketcompany.com for more resources and coaching.

ISBN: 978-0-9903219-1-0

© 2014 Casey Graham and The Rocket Company

Writers: Casey Graham and Ben Crawshaw
Lead Editor: Holly Crawshaw
Creative Direction: Holly Crawshaw and Jill Walker
Design: Brian Manley at Fun With Robots Design Co.

Printed in the United States of America

Molding Box
2625 South 600 West
Salt Lake City, Utah 84115 U.S.A.
moldingbox.com

Dedicated To . . .

My wife, Kacie. You have seen me at my best and at my worst, and your love has remained unconditional. You're the most incredible mom and wife I have ever seen, and this book exists because of your unwavering support.

My beautiful and generous daughter, Darby. Your big dreams inspire me to dream big, too.

And, finally, my joyful son, Gage. Thank you for always bringing laughter and personality to our family.

CONTENTS

INTRODUCTION
THE END OF FUNDRAISING AS YOU KNOW IT

Most Money Raising Advice Makes Things Too Complicated VII

Anybody Can Raise Money For Anything IX

Raising Money Through Lemonade Stands Is Not That Different From Raising Money For Million-Dollar Organizations XIII

The One-Page Method To Help Anybody Raise Money For Anything XV

SECTION I
THE ONE-PAGE PLAN
STEP ONE: OWN IT

1. If You Don't Own It, No One Will 1
2. Why Somebody Becomes Nobody When Raising Money 5
3. Excuses Are Lies That Keep You Broke 9
4. People Will Not Hate You For Asking For Money 13

SECTION II
THE ONE-PAGE PLAN
STEP TWO: CLARIFY IT

5. Clarity Creates Certainty, And Certain People Take Massive Action 21
6. How Much Money Do You Need And By When? 27
7. Tell The World How Much Money You Will Raise And By When 31

SECTION III
THE ONE-PAGE PLAN
STEP THREE: PLAN IT

8. Passion Is Better With A Plan 39
9. Ingredient One: A Compelling Story 43
10. Ingredient Two: A Concrete Calendar 47
11. Ingredient Three: An On-Board Team 51
12. Ingredient Four: A Targeted Audience 55
13. Ingredient Five: A Targeted Message 59
14. Ingredient Six: An Easy Way To Give 63

SECTION IV
THE ONE-PAGE PLAN
STEP FOUR: DO IT

15. 1 Ask Trumps 1,000 Hints 69
16. Asking Privately > Asking Publicly 73
17. Why A Specific Ask Beats A General Ask 79

18. Ask One To Make Two 83

19. Ask Donors To Give To Deadlines 87

20. Create A List Of People To Ask 91

SECTION V
THE ONE-PAGE PLAN
STEP FIVE:
CELEBRATE IT

21. Remember: They Funded Your Dream 97

22. 10 Creative Ways To Say "Thank You" 101

CONCLUSION
YOU CAN CHANGE
THE WORLD

Think Big. Act Small. 109

INTRODUCTION
THE END OF FUNDRAISING AS YOU KNOW IT

THE #1 REASON PEOPLE FAIL AT FUNDING THEIR DREAM

On April 27, 2011, 212 tornados ripped through Alabama, tearing the state apart. The damage was disturbing and overwhelming. One of the places affected was my hometown of Pleasant Grove. The street where I grew up was turned inside out. I later learned that the twister was an F-5, the biggest possible.

In Alabama and surrounding states, the storm killed 324 people. Men and women I went to high school with died. People I grew up knowing all my life were gone. Lives were lost, homes were lost, and hope was lost. As I watched the news, I thought, *Those are my people.* I knew I had to do something.

I was facing a couple of problems. One, I was in Georgia. Two, I was recovering from foot surgery; I was confined to either the couch or bed. I felt helpless. How could I help my hometown when I couldn't even stand or walk? But I kept repeating the words *go* and *help* in my mind. I couldn't go to Alabama. But I could help by raising money.

I'm not a professional fundraiser. I don't own a bunch of books on raising money. I don't have a degree in raising money. But I said to myself,

"I have to do what I can." So, I set a goal of raising $10,000.

I went straight to technology. I sent emails. I sent texts. I utilized social media. Within hours $10,000 was on its way to help my hometown. With every dollar that came in I had the same thoughts: *Those are my people. I have to do something.*

With the help of a lot of people cooler and smarter than me, we raised $203,000 in a few weeks. The support was overwhelming. Some big donors made our jaws drop. Fantastic things happened through some really amazing people. And I learned something that changed me: **I can make a difference!** Me, a redneck from Alabama on bed rest.

Now, I'm certainly not saying the fundraiser was about me. In fact, it happened despite my insecurities. I kept telling myself that people didn't want to be bothered by Casey Graham. In return, people kept giving money to help the relief efforts.

I also learned that **money can make the difference.** Money can fuel the aid that needs to be provided after a tragedy. But money isn't just for tragedies or disasters. Money is used to start businesses, save enslaved children, kick-start albums, or pay for your dinner. Money is a big deal.

> **THE #1 REASON PEOPLE FAIL AT RAISING MONEY IS THAT RAISING MONEY IS HARD.**

After I raised over $203,000 in a matter of weeks, I stopped and asked myself: "What just happened? What part of my method made it possible for me to raise this much money?" My answer that day didn't reveal to me that I had cracked a code for raising money. However, after it happened time and time again, I noticed that the steps were the same. As long as I kept repeating them, they worked.

Around this same time, I also started noticing *failed* attempts to raise money. I saw people begging for money through mass emails, Facebook, and Kickstarter projects. I watched as they struggled to get the money they needed.

The truth is, more people fail at raising money than succeed. And there's a reason for that:

The #1 reason people fail at raising money is that raising money is *hard.*

INTRODUCTION

I'm a genius, right? I know that isn't a monumental realization for you, but it's vital to keep in mind. Raising money is hard.

The other day my daughter decided that she wanted to raise money for kids with cancer. It was her dream. I asked, "What do you want to do to raise this money?" She quickly responded, "Open a lemonade stand!" So I helped her set it up, and I sat outside while she tried to sell lemonade.

Let me first state that my daughter is a beautiful six-year-old girl. There is no purer heart on Earth. She had no intention of keeping any of the money for herself. And in my subdivision—a normal Atlanta suburb—people have the money. They have enough change rattling around in their ashtrays. They can buy a glass of lemonade.

I counted the cars that drove by. Not a good idea. Only 2 out of the first 10 stopped. The rest drove right past my daughter's charming lemonade stand. I got surprisingly angry. I wanted to punch people in the face. At one point, I considered offering specific hand gestures to people who refused to stop. I appreciate the filter that seized that idea.

If only 2 out of 10 people will buy my adorable daughter's lemonade—*which helps cancer patients and only costs a quarter*—how in the world is anyone supposed to raise money for anything anywhere? How are you supposed to raise money for your new building? For your staff's salaries? For your business expansion? To film your movie? To pay your bills? To get your message out? To put on your event?

The truth is, extracting money from people's pockets is difficult. And because of that, most people who try will fail.

I tested this theory. My friend, Michael, and I were driving one day when we saw a guy standing on the side of the road. Michael asked me, "Do you think that guy will give me a dollar?" I found myself completely interested in that challenge. Out of that scenario our *Will You Give Me a Dollar?* campaign was born.

We asked that simple question home and abroad: 10 states and 3 countries. We used a lot of different tests and methods. You know what we found out?

Most people say no.

I'm not talking about a lot of money here. I'm talking about a buck. That's less than a cup of coffee. Heck, that's less than a bad cup of coffee! Still, most people did—and will—say no.

The amount of money you are trying to raise doesn't matter. Whether you're trying to raise a buck or $100,000, it's difficult.

After this experience, I began looking back. I thought about the people I coached who were successful at funding their dreams. And when I did, I discovered a very distinct, repeatable pattern.

In the 1990s there was a popular Nintendo game called Contra that I played constantly. Even as I type this, nostalgia is overwhelming me. Man, I loved that game. And yet, at the same time, I hated it. Because I couldn't conquer it. As much as I played—and as much as I watched my friends beat that game—I still couldn't do it. There were certain levels I simply could not pass.

My failure only seemed to fuel my passion for Contra. Okay, maybe obsession is a better word than passion. But despite my crazy ambition to beat Contra, my gaming never elevated to elite Contra status.

Then one day, my friends and I learned something. Something life-changing. Earth-shattering. History-making. Something that would forever change my Contra-playing future. It went like this:

UP, UP, DOWN, DOWN, LEFT, RIGHT, LEFT, RIGHT, B, A, B, A, SELECT, START.

At least that's how I remember it. With that formula, I had endless lives at my disposal!

And even though I knew I was cheating the system, it did not minimize my satisfaction at conquering the game. That simple code, when repeated, allowed me to beat Contra every time I played it.

And that's how raising money works (minus the cheating-the-system part). People who do well at raising money know something that others don't. They know a code. When I connected the dots and discovered a code for raising money, I realized that the code was superior to passion, strategizing, originality, and coolness. I know people who have all of these features but still fail at raising money.

INTRODUCTION

When it comes to raising money, most people just do what they know. That's what I did when I played Contra without the code. And I was a good Contra player. But I wasn't good enough.

When people see a Facebook campaign that seemed to work, they do that. When non-profits see a project campaign that met its goal, they do that. When people see a business model that made money for an entrepreneur, they do that. People assume that whatever worked for someone else will work for them. That's why they fail. When it comes to raising money, I suggest you don't do what the industry standard suggests or what everyone else thinks you should do.

And yes, that will be hard. That's the bad news. But here's the good news: **whatever is at stake, it's worth it.**

Think about it. Most people are raising money to do good. To make something, someone, or someplace better. They want to use money to make the world a better place, or put their family in a better position. Whether it's PTA moms, start-up businesses, lemonade stands for cancer, or a non-profit to help addicts, betterment is the goal.

That's your dream: doing something better.

Raising money is hard, but it's not impossible. Inside this book, there's something different called *The One-Page Plan for Raising Money*. In a few short chapters, I'm going to show you exactly how to do this.

Learning to raise money is like solving a Rubik's cube. You can come up with a strategy. You can practice for days and years. You can even throw the dang thing against the wall. And you'll never figure out how to solve it. But when you learn the pattern of turns, you can beat a Rubik's cube over and over again. And look awesome doing it. You know, impress the ladies. Possibly. Or possibly not.

I can promise you this: If your idea is foolish or selfish, it probably won't flourish. But if it's not, *The One-Page Plan* will work every time. It's as simple as earning unlimited lives with the repeating Contra pattern.

MOST MONEY-RAISING ADVICE MAKES THINGS TOO COMPLICATED

I just spent an hour and a half on Amazon.com. I love that website. 1-click shopping? Are you kidding me? What a terrible and awesome idea! After an hour of shopping for University of Alabama football gear (Roll Tide!), I finally remembered why I was on that site—to look for books on raising money.

Now, I may be a simple country boy from Alabama, but I've read a number of books on business and finance. And when skimming through the search results on fundraising books, I had significant trouble understanding some of the ideas and terminology. To be completely honest, they might as well be written in a different language. Professionals write fundraising books full of fundraising plans that I can't understand.

And that's a problem. Because **complicated strategies kill fundraising.**

I remember taking Trigonometry in high school. Yikes, who doesn't? I had no business taking that class. But I was in love with a girl who took it. That's how I was in high school. I didn't get crushes on girls—I just went ahead and fell flat-on-my-face in love with them. You would think girls would love a guy like me: admittedly passionate. They didn't.

Anyway, when it came time to actually *do* Trig, I would stare at the questions, problems, equations—whatever you call them. I felt paralyzed. There were so many steps. So many ways to approach the problem. I didn't know how to start. So, guess what broke down? My commitment to Trig (not my commitment to Miss Two-Seats-Ahead).

Let me throw another one at you. Have you ever looked at your house after you threw a party or cooked a huge meal? You stare at it, wrecked kitchen and all, and think, *I have no idea where to start.* You could start with the sink and the dishes. But who wants to do that? So, you start gathering trash. But that's too overwhelming and messy. So, for those of you without OCD, you just go to bed. Isn't that a great feeling—when you decide you're going to sleep instead of tackling the mess? What a great night's sleep that provides! What you've done is procrastinated because you didn't know where to start. Complexity killed your commitment to clean your house.

But that's exactly what I'm trying to avoid in this book. *The One-Page Plan* is simple. It's systematic. It's formulaic. Not Trigonometry-formulaic, but you-can-understand-it formulaic. You won't look at it and wonder where to start. All the mental work is done for you. I've taken the guesswork out. Why? Because I want you to be committed to raising money. Complexity will kill that commitment. But clarity will allow you to take action.

There are professional books or blogs that will weigh you down with details. They will give you multifaceted strategies. But what you don't need is more strategies—strategies come and go. **You need a tested and true method.**

ANYBODY CAN RAISE MONEY FOR ANYTHING

I told you earlier about my daughter, Darby, and her attempt to sell lemonade to help kids with cancer. To be more specific, the money was designated to allow kids with cancer to go on a special vacation with their families. How cool is that?

Darby's cousin, Emma, heard about it and said, "I want to do that, too." Her plan was to sell rubber band bracelets. Her goal was to raise $100. She posted some pics on my Instagram account. She shot a short video and asked me to tweet it. In 48 hours, Emma raised $170.

Emma kept it simple. She got right to the point. She had a clear goal. She owned the process. That's what made Emma—a nine-year-old kid—successful at raising money.

The truth about raising money is that it *should* be that simple. In fact, **if a kid can't understand your plan for raising money, then it's too complicated.** That's what makes *The One-Page Plan* so great. It's simple. Foolproof. Anybody who does exactly what it says will raise money. I promise.

Recently, I sat down with an incredible couple whose dream was to move with their three children to Costa Rica for missions work. At the time we met, they had 45 days to raise $45,000. They had passion and drive, but they couldn't decide which of the thousands of fundraisers they should choose. Write letters? Update Facebook statuses? Wash cars?

They were utilizing a social media campaign but had experienced little success. I told them that seventy percent of the money they needed would come from people they knew personally. I helped them understand that more money can be raised off *direct* messages, *private* Facebook messages, and *individual* text messages. In other words:

$1 Given > 1,000 Retweets

Less than an hour after our meeting, I got a text from the husband that said: "Thank you so much, dude! Just got someone to match $250 and we haven't even made it back home yet."

This couple **came into that meeting knowing that they weren't professional fundraisers. They came out knowing that it didn't matter.** Listen, if raising money were only for the pros, we'd all be in trouble. There are only a select group of people who have an interest in raising money for a living. Even fewer are specifically trained to do it. If you're reading this book and you're a trained professional, you're probably mad because I haven't (and I won't) say anything deep or profound. I'm sorry. I give you permission to write a scathing blog about me to let off some steam. But I simply cannot escape this simple truth:

Anybody can raise money for anything.

All you have to do is ask.

Anybody can raise money to fund their dream, but few people believe it. People say they can't. They're not "wired that way." It makes them uncomfortable. They don't want to be like the TV preacher with crazy hair who asks for money in exchange for a holy tissue. But in order to be successful, you don't have to be a natural. And you certainly don't *want* to be creepy or greedy. All you *need* to do is ask.

Years ago, a client of mine founded a non-profit that helps teenage girls with unplanned pregnancies. She had never raised a large sum of money in her entire life. In fact, since the organization's formation, she

INTRODUCTION

had only raised $30,000.

When I spoke with with her, I explained the principles behind what would become *The One-Page Plan*. She responded immediately. Within 30 days, she raised $31,000 (it was 28 days, to be exact). She raised more money in one month than she had in the history of the non-profit.

Simplicity is the key to fundraising because there are so many options out there. So many things you *could* do. So many approaches you could take. It's paralyzing to look at a list of golf tournaments, sales events, and social media announcements. I think people don't need to be overwhelmed by what they could do. They need to focus on what they *should* do.

PASSIONATE PEOPLE STIR PASSION IN OTHERS.

Here's some hopeful news for you: **Everybody has *somebody* that would give them money.** I would even go as far as saying that everybody has somebodies that would give them money. Over the next few sections, I'll help you figure out who those people are and how to ask them to give.

The reality is that no one has ever said: "Man, I hated giving to that good person. I hated helping that business get on its feet. I hated supporting that awesome organization. I hated sending my money to make the world a better place. I hated funding the dream that changed someone's life." After you get over the initial anxiety of asking people to give, it's not actually that challenging to raise funds. Passionate people stir passion in others. And that passion will lead people to give to your cause.

No, not *everybody* will give. But *somebody* will.

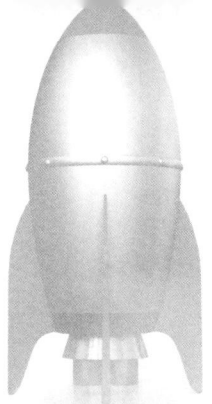

RAISING MONEY THROUGH LEMONADE STANDS IS NOT THAT DIFFERENT FROM RAISING MONEY FOR MILLION-DOLLAR ORGANIZATIONS

I calculated the other day that I have worked with over 5,000 clients. I'm not sure why I calculated that. I guess that's what numbers people do. I've experienced success with almost all 5,000 clients. I've helped my daughter and her friends raise money through lemonade stands, and I've helped million-dollar organizations raise ridiculous amounts of money. I don't say that to brag or to be arrogant. At the same time, I don't think you want to read a book by a guy who hasn't succeeded.

I really, *really* like helping people. And not because it's good for business. No, it's because I really do like it. If you haven't, you should help somebody and see how it feels. You'll probably like it, too. I liked helping people long before it became my business.

So, like I said, I've seen plenty of people fund their dreams. But it didn't always happen. I've seen clients fail. Almost all of them had one thing in common: they told me their idea was different.

Let me stop right there. For the record, I think it's awesome when people feel like their idea is different. It gets me fired up. But when that's the reason they refuse to work *The One-Page Plan*, I get a little defensive. Not because I have a pride issue—I don't care if people think my plan's stupid, don't feel like doing it, or think I'm a just a country boy from Alabama (which is true). I just don't want people to use "my-idea-is-different" as an excuse to not put in the time and work needed to execute a legitimate fundraising plan.

Dan Kennedy, a guy I really respect, says that thinking your business or idea is just "different" is the rally cry of the broke. Even if your idea is the greatest idea in the world. Even if you've seen someone with a similar idea raise money without a plan. Even if you've seen someone with a different plan raise money for a similar idea. It's still not an excuse. You need a plan that's been tested. And you need to execute it.

With seven billion people in the world, wouldn't it be safe to assume that someone has thought of your idea before? I don't want to squelch your optimism. On the contrary, I want to fuel your dreams. And I simply think that saying your idea is different is more of an obstacle than a launchpad.

Listen, even if your idea *is* different, you still need to clearly explain it. You still need a plan. You still need to ask people for money. And you still need to make them *want* to give it to you. As a side note, if your idea is too different, that could actually create problems for people. It's the reason why it's hard to get funding for new inventions. And it's the reason why some "As Seen on TV" products are only seen on infomercials at three in the morning. As much as I love AromaTrim ("smell your way into weight loss") and Ronco Spray-on Hair, sometimes an idea that "no one else has heard of" is just, well, weird.

In the end, your idea is probably a good idea. More than that, it's your passion. But whether it's a lemonade stand, a million-dollar organization, or a business proposal that no one has thought of before, you still need a plan.

And I would love it (and you will too once you try it) if that plan were *The One-Page Plan*!

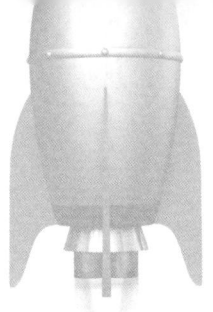

THE ONE-PAGE METHOD TO HELP ANYBODY RAISE MONEY FOR ANYTHING

In my organization, we work with a wide range of clients—churches, businesses, non-profits, kids with lemonade stands, etc. We'll meet with just about anybody.

Last year, we helped a group of churches raise over six million dollars in one day. Maybe that sounds like a lot to you. Or maybe it actually sounds unimpressive. My company saw it as a huge win.

This one-day, six million dollar venture began with a decision we made to test our theory. We had a code for raising money. And we wanted to see if our code would work in one of the most diverse markets in existence—churches.

You may know nothing about the church world. That's okay. I started attending church at age 17. And I quickly learned that they can be weird. And random. And selective. If you don't go to church, you probably think they're all alike. I used to think that. Now, I don't think any two are the same. We work with a church in Illinois called Guiding Star of the Sun. First off, how cool is that name? We also work with First Baptist of Small Town, USA, and the Universalist Life Church of Mother Goose Laying an Egg. Okay, I made up those last two names.

We work with Catholic churches and non-denominational churches. We work with churches full of old people and churches full of young, hip singles. Yes, I just used the word "hip" in my book (I thought about writing "hipster," but I figured that would be too much). We have churches where the preacher sits on a throne, and churches where the pastor looks like Glenn Danzig of The Misfits (you may have to look that one up).

Here's my point. In our experience with these unique, diverse churches, there was one common thread. They all needed money.

We had over 200 churches take part in our one-day drive. It was scheduled to begin 90 days before Christmas. We assured each church, "We'll coach you. It all boils down to our code. Keep it simple. Keep it clear. And keep it action-oriented."

So, they entered the code. And they raised six million dollars in a day.

This code is the simplest way we know to raise money. Professionals create complex systems. But I'm not into complexity. I'm into do-ability. I believe this is for anyone who wants to raise money for anything. It's easy to understand. And, as we proved, it works.

Remember back-to-school shopping as a kid? Some of you are kids, so you don't have to dig too deep in your memory banks. Some of you are parents and have taken your kids recently. I hated school shopping. I remember asking my mom why we needed all this crap. She didn't like me saying the word *crap*. But she also didn't have a good answer to my question. What mom on planet Earth can explain to her 10-year-old son the purpose of a protractor? She did, however, buy me a Transformers Trapper Keeper. That's the equivalent these days to a 10-year-old with an iPhone. I was the coolest kid in town.

If I took you back-to-school shopping to prepare you for raising money, here's the list of supplies I'd buy you:

One sheet of paper.

That's all you need. On that sheet of paper you need the five components that make up the code to raising money. I'm going to give you a quick overview of them in this chapter. You're going to be tempted not to read the rest of the book. Don't do that. Getting all of this information is the difference between raising a little cash and com-

INTRODUCTION

pletely funding your dream. The next few pages tell you what. The rest of the book tells you how.

STEP #1

The old way of thinking says, "I hope somebody raises the money." I've heard that a thousand times. The CEO or executive director blames the board members. The board blames the director. Everybody points fingers. Nobody raises a cent.

Or we see something bad happen. And we say, "Man, somebody should organize something to help them." But we do nothing personally. I used to say that. Then I realized, who is this elusive "Somebody" we keep referring to? Somebody wasn't paying my mortgage, washing my car, or changing my kid's diaper. To prove my point, one day I said out loud, "*Somebody* should change my kid's diaper!" My wife looked at me with that "another-check-in-the-idiot-column-for-you" look. She doesn't give me that look often . . . that I notice. So when I get it, I know I've really earned it. I immediately went and changed my daughter's diaper. And while I did, I had this thought about tragedies and bad things happening (yes, I think about tragedies when I change diapers). **Somebody becomes nobody really fast when it comes to raising money.**

The new way of thinking says: "**I will make this happen.** If I don't own the outcome, the outcome will never come. This is MY job, come hell or high water. I will see this through. The money IS going to be raised."

I want to teach you the power of ownership. The problem is people want to rent a vision. They don't want to buy it.

When my daughter decided that she wanted a lemonade stand, she *really* decided it. Meaning, she wouldn't freaking drop it. She kept bringing it up, and I kept putting her off. I told her it was too rainy, too windy, too overcast. One day, I told her that the barometer was dropping, so we needed to wait. I had no idea what the barometer was, still don't. It's not that I didn't want to help my daughter. Honestly, I was just being lazy.

On the first sunny day, however, I knew it was time. So, I walked outside with my awesome little girl and set up the lemonade stand. And while I did, I had a couple of thoughts: One, *I love this girl more than life itself.* Two, *I just got owned by my daughter!* She took ownership. She made it her job to make it happen.

Ask yourself: Do I own it? Am I that person?

STEP #2

The old way of raising money is kind of mythical. It says, "I hope it will happen sometime soon." But **sometime soon gets us nowhere fast.** This is true for all areas of our lives—exercise, home improvement, catching up with old friends. Someday usually equals no day.

You have to clarify the goal. You have to pick a day and a dollar amount. I know this sounds easy. You're wondering how in the world I'm going to write an entire section on this. But most businesses and organizations can't define those variables. They don't know what they need and by when. They're just hoping it will all work out.

Did you know that you can *hope* your way into failure? For some reason, I have a vivid memory of being at my friend's house in high school. We were hanging out, playing music, staring at his black-lit Marilyn Manson posters. Creepy, right? I remember thinking about how cool all the possibilities in life were. But I wasn't *doing* anything. I was just sitting and hoping. And playing my guitar.

That may be an extreme example, but you can easily find yourself in the same situation (minus the traumatizing Manson posters). You can find yourself sitting around thinking of what could be and how cool the possibilities are. **But dreaming is not equal to doing.**

The new way tells you to **pick a date and dollar amount and stick to it.**

STEP #3

The old way says, "I'll figure it out as I go." This is a typical fundraising mindset—just wing it. Most people are passionate about their cause. But because they're not professionally trained in raising money, their

INTRODUCTION

passion doesn't come with a plan. And that, unfortunately, is usually a dead-end street. Every time I'm face-to-face with somebody in that boat, I tell them this corny phrase: **passion without a plan equals pain.**

In the world of raising money, people are far more likely to give when there's a plan in place. People who have a plan do exponentially better than those who wing it. Fundraising is a lot like flying a plane—the bigger the plane, the longer the runway should be. If your goal is large, your plan should give you ample margin to accomplish it.

STEP #4

The old way says, "Dodge it." Dodge asking people for money. Not too long ago, I went to breakfast with a guy who wanted to talk about his non-profit. He talked for an hour. He kept hinting that he'd like me to give money, but he never came out and clearly said it. At the end of his spiel, I point-blank asked him if he wanted me to give him some money. Even then he fumbled, implied, and danced around. So I asked him again. He finally admitted, "Yes, I'd love for you to give." So I gave! Thank goodness the suspense was over! But if I had never come out and asked him what he was hinting at, I never would've known he wanted me to give.

Not asking directly is the same as not asking at all.

I know this is hard for some people. I know it takes a lot of courage. But one thing I can promise you: Fundraising Rocket wants to help—with this book, and with the resources we are giving you **(at FundraisingRocket.com/tools)**. We'll give you some really practical phrases. And we'll teach you how to ask directly.

STEP #5

The old way says, "Once it's over, forget about it." When we're done with our fundraising, the temptation is to not look back. After all, progress is great and we need to keep moving forward.

The new way reminds us that **saying "thank you" creates repeat givers.** Not only that, it's simply the right thing to do. If somebody gives you a dollar, you thank them for that dollar. Mass texts, tweets, and Facebook messages aren't enough.

Individual expressions of appreciation don't go unnoticed. A handwritten thank-you card. A personalized text. A phone call to say "thanks." All of these methods make your gratitude personal and meaningful.

Having walked you through an overview, it's time to dive into the one-page fundraising plan.

It's time to enter the code and take the steps to fund your dream.

Let's go!

SECTION I

**THE ONE-PAGE PLAN
STEP ONE: OWN IT**

CHAPTER 1

IF YOU DON'T OWN IT, NO ONE WILL

When I started The Rocket Company, I drove around in a red truck. And I'm not talking about *any* red truck. I'm talking about the most awesome red truck to ever be driven in the history of the universe! She was a five-speed, 1998 Ford Ranger. Outwardly, she looked great. Inwardly, she was nasty. I'm talking *nasty*. In high school, my friends and I would pile in my impressive (and at that time, brand new) red truck after baseball practice in our filthy, sweaty uniforms. Over time, my brand new seats had butt sweat stains. That's gross when you're my age. But you don't even think about it when you're a high school guy. By the way, I never thought I would use the phrase "butt sweat stains" in my book.

There's another thing that gave this truck personality and endeared it to my heart—I used to be redheaded . . . back when I had hair. Man, I miss those days! So, there I was. A redhead in a red truck. Looking sexy. Launching a new company. Driving around. Making cold calls. Trying to help churches raise money. Livin' the dream!

Here was my strategy. I would pull up to a church in my awesome red truck, march into the office and find the secretary. By the way, most businesses and churches don't call them secretaries anymore. They call them administrative assistants. But it was a common job title back in the day. So, I'd strike up a conversation with the secretary and ask if there was a person on staff who would agree to let me help them raise money.

Needless to say, my first year of business didn't quite line up with my initial fantasies of success. My company went into debt to the tune of $80,000. I missed a lot of my daughter's functions and events. And I could barely keep food on the table. But hey, I still had my awesome red truck, right? Well, only because my dad paid it off back in '98. As long as I made enough money to afford gas (which I didn't have all the time), she kept cranking up and driving along! But she certainly didn't drive me to a lot of successful meetings.

I honestly think the only reason people hired me in the early stages of my company was because they felt sorry for me, which I'm very grateful for.

It was in this start-up stage that I met a guy in the process of planting a church in a suburb of Atlanta. For those of you who have no idea what the heck "planting a church" means, don't worry. I had no idea for most of my life (if you would've asked, I would've guessed it was a cult that brainwashes people through plants and drugs). It's actually a lot like starting a new business or non-profit. There's a "cause," and that cause needs money to operate. You'd think church workers are great at asking for money because of television preachers. The truth is, church workers are terrible at asking for money *because* of television preachers. No one wants to sound like one.

This guy was no different. He was struggling. He had zero dollars in the bank. His church's cash flow wasn't meeting their budget forecast. In fact, he didn't even have enough money to pay for my company's services. So, I told him the same thing I told many pastors at that time: "It's free until you can pay me." I'm not even sure what that means, but that's what I told him.

One day he said, "I can pay you now." *Thank the Lord,* I thought. We launched into a discussion about our plan to help his church raise more money. At one point in that conversation, he admitted that he wasn't receiving a paycheck that month.

"Why?" I asked.

"Because," he responded, "I used my paycheck to pay you."

I felt awful. Just terrible. Don't get me wrong, I *really* needed the money. But I hated the idea that my paycheck deprived this man of his. But I learned something about him that day—he was finally ready to get help. Like most scenarios in life, **when you really need help, you become willing to make a personal investment.** Those are the moments when you or I will see a counselor, meet with a trainer, hire a life coach, or do whatever we need to do to make a difference. In that moment, I knew this pastor would succeed.

In fact, the last time I talked to him, he had months of financial margin in the bank. And here's the simple reason why. He understood that **if he didn't take personal ownership of what he was raising money for, no one would.**

Most people don't make that decision. They *hope* that someone will raise the money. They *hope* that a big donor will come along. They *hope* that a miracle will drop cash into their lives. That's where this pastor was when I met him—hoping that things would change and people would start giving more. Unfortunately, hope is the slow death of a fundraising dream. You don't need to have more hope. You need to take more steps. That's what this section will drive you toward—taking your first big step.

When this man got to the point that he was willing to give up his paycheck to see his vision through, he crossed the immeasurable divide between *I hope* and *I will*. He took matters into his own hands. He owned it. And he started raising money to fund his dreams.

It's equal to a comparison of renting a house and owning it. There's a different level of care. I've been a tenant before. Whenever I heard noises that didn't sound right, saw cracks in the ceiling, or felt water in places it didn't belong, I thought, *Man I'm so glad that problem—whatever it is—doesn't belong to me.*

On the other hand, I've been a landlord. When my renters called to tell me that something was broken, I hated it. Dread overtook my soul. But you know what I did? I got off the couch, drove to the gas station to buy some Runts® and a Mountain Dew®, then went to the rental house and fixed it. I made it right. Why? Because I'm the *owner*.

When you are the owner of a dream or a vision, you will take on the full mantle of responsibility. When you're a renter, you can pass on the responsibility whenever times get tough or something goes wrong.

Don't rent the vision of raising money. When you get tired or people tell you "no," don't quit. One of the core phrases in our company is **think like an owner.** An owner won't quit until it's done. They may fail, but they will get up and try again.

Professionals will tell you to start with a mission statement. I will tell you to start with a decision. Decide to own it. And at the end of this section, I'm going to ask you to do something that will make your ownership official. You will be one step closer to funding your dreams.

Is what you're raising money for worth it? That family? That cause? Your business? Cancer research? If you think it's worth the money, then it's worth it for you to own it. Because **if you don't own the outcome, the outcome will own you.**

It all comes down to one big idea: *I will.* Not we *will* or *they will.* But I will. When you say *I will,* it will happen for you!

CHAPTER 2

WHY SOMEBODY BECOMES NOBODY WHEN RAISING MONEY

When natural disasters strike, I get a lot of messages. People text me, tweet me, Facebook me, email me, etc. At some point in the message or conversation, I inevitably read this phrase: "Somebody should raise money for these people in need."

Honestly, I think most people are hoping that I'll raise the money. And I'm okay with that. I feel honored that people think of me when they become aware of big needs. But for a lot of reasons, it's not always possible. So, I typically respond with a short and simple question:

Why don't YOU raise the money?

When I ask that question, I'm not trying to be sarcastic. And I'm not trying to avoid the responsibility. I simply want to know their answer. The crazy thing is that most people are totally surprised by my comeback. It's as if it never even crossed their minds that they could lead the charge. It was in one of those interactions that I decided to write this book. Because I really do believe in people. And I really am confident that anybody can raise money for anything. Especially if their intentions are good. And *especially* if they follow *The One-Page Plan*.

The phrase *somebody should* is commonplace. In the culture I live in, I hear it all the time:
- "The government should do something about that."
- "That school should fix that problem."
- "A local business should take that on as a project."
- "Somebody should start that business."
- "This is an issue that more people should get involved with."

Here's what I want to ask you to do: **be the somebody.** Just do it. Just be it! That business, need or cause that you feel passionate about—that you can't get off your mind—take a step toward *being* the answer. I believe you can!

I also believe this: **somebody becomes nobody when it comes to raising money.** *Somebody* should means *nobody will.*

I used to work in an organization where my co-workers and I were always coming up with new ideas. If you walked around our office or sat in one of our staff meetings, you'd consistently hear phrases like: "We should try this." "We should create a new system." "We should send this new email." "We should rally our community around this idea." I think we convinced ourselves that we were the smartest staff in the country. Inspired by our newest Apple product purchases, we all thought we were little Steve Jobs juniors. Starbucks in hand? Check. Trendy jeans on? Check. Ready to change the world? You better believe it!

Our boss—who also loved Apple products, Starbucks coffee and trendy jeans—would always respond, "That's a great idea. But *we* doesn't have an office." We'd stare blankly at him. He'd continue, "Which one of you is personally willing to take on this idea and make it happen?" That's when we'd get it. "We" doesn't work here—a bunch of individuals do. And for our brilliant idea to come to maturity, one of us needs to run with it.

When it comes to new ideas that need fundraising, here's my modification of my former boss's statement: "That's a great idea. But *somebody* doesn't have an office. Are *you* personally willing to take this idea on and make it happen?"

STEP ONE: OWN IT

I have a friend named Blake Canterbury who gets this. Blake is way cooler than me. He goes to all the trendy parties in downtown Atlanta. He has awesome hair. He even wears cool tank tops. Me? I drive a minivan around the suburbs. I'm bald. If I wear a tank top, it's because . . . well . . . I guess there's *never* a good reason for me to wear a tank top!

But Blake isn't just cool. He's smart. A few years back, Blake became increasingly aware of people's needs in Atlanta. Instead of saying "somebody should do something to help these people," Blake decided to be a personal conduit between their problems and the solutions.

In 2009, Blake founded beremedy, a company that uses social media to help people. Blake leverages Twitter, Facebook, and Instagram to broadcast current needs to his large (and growing) audience of followers. For example, if someone needs a bed, Blake will get on social media and ask if anyone has an extra bed they can spare. Or he'll ask if anyone is willing to give money to buy a new bed. Often, the need is met within minutes. Not only did Blake make a decision to own the needs of others, he built a company that allows other people to have ownership, too. Brilliant, right? If you're like me, the first emotion you have when you observe beremedy is jealousy: *Why didn't I think of that? It's such a simple yet brilliant concept.* With my bald head and my minivan, I probably couldn't have pulled it off.

The good news is that if you're reading this book, you've probably decided to be the somebody. If you've taken the step to own it, you're on the right track. I can't tell you how excited (and how proud) that makes me! What you've done is crucial. You've decided: I am the somebody. I will personally own this. I will make this happen. And that's the first step toward successfully raising money.

CHAPTER 3

EXCUSES ARE LIES THAT KEEP YOU BROKE

The other day I sat down with a guy who had an incredible dream for a business. He's an awesome dude. Talented. Smart. Successful. He had some great ideas. And he was passionate about them. But over tomato soup and blackened fish (which was delicious, by the way), he told me all the reasons why he couldn't ask people for money: "It's not my gifting. I'm scared it will make people mad. I'm not wired to ask for donations."

As he talked, one thought kept running through my mind: *As great as this guy is, if he keeps making excuses, he's going to stay broke.*

He made a lot of deposits into his vision by explaining his ideas. By articulating how his ideas would help people. And by dreaming up the results. But he also made a lot of withdrawals from his vision by making excuses for why he wouldn't ask people for money. Unfortunately, **when you make more withdrawals than deposits, you end up with a broke vision.**

I see this a lot when it comes to raising money—people who rob their vision of momentum. They aren't bad people. They aren't even necessarily negative people. Many of them are great people (like the guy I met for that delicious blackened fish). And many of their excuses are valid. But as long as they allow their excuses to stand in the way of raising money, they will remain broke.

A couple of weeks ago, I attended my daughter's kindergarten orientation. I noticed that the PTA was raising money. And I'm glad they were. What they were raising money for was really important. Now, I've had numerous conversations with PTA groups throughout the years. And after a while, all their excuses sound the same: "Only a few parents actually help. No one seems motivated to get involved. The school doesn't offer any support." Those reasons may be true and valid. But most PTAs respond like the one at my daughter's school. They don't put forth much effort. They sit behind a table and hope people will walk up and hand them money. And even though their cause is important, they've let too many excuses make too many withdrawals from their vision.

As I talk with people who have a dream they want to fund, there are some excuses that I hear more than others. Here are eight of the most common:

1. *I don't know where to start.* This is an example of a valid excuse. When I ventured into raising money for the first time, I didn't know where to start either. **But not *knowing* where to start shouldn't stop you from *figuring* out where to start.** Don't stop because you don't know. That will most definitely keep you broke.

2. *I'm not gifted to do this.* Listen, not many people are "gifted" at asking other people for money. There may be people out there who are better at it than you, but that's probably because they've practiced. They've discovered what works for them, and they've done it over and over. Oh yeah, and they've refused to give up.

3. *I'm not good with all the technology stuff.* This statement comes from people who don't like, or aren't familiar with, things like Facebook, Twitter, Instagram, blogging, or other social media resources. The truth is, **people were successful at raising money long before social media came along.** There are other ways. Or, here's another idea: learn something new! Get online. Give it a shot. You're not going to hurt yourself or blow something up.

4. *I tried it, and it didn't work.* This is like saying you put your pinkie toe in the water, it was too cold, so you refuse to ever get

STEP ONE: OWN IT

in the water again. So, you tried to sell Krispy Kreme donuts one weekend and you didn't hit your fundraising goal. It's not a reason to quit. Here's what I know—**there are very few ideas that people won't fund.** If you have the right plan in place, it's almost impossible to fail.

Most people who fail at raising money do so because their *method* is flawed, not their idea. When a toddler is learning to walk and he or she falls down and hits the floor, it's not the floor's fault. It's their method of walking and balancing. But toddlers will fall, flip, hit the wall, bump their heads, skin their knees *until* they get the hang of it. You and I can learn a lot from them. **We need to become *until* people.** We need to commit to trying *until* it's done. We need to keep asking *until* the money is raised.

5. *People will get mad at me.* This is such a big deal that we'll spend an entire chapter talking about it later. But for now I'll give you my short response: **the people who get mad at you for raising money are not the right people to care about.** I'm not saying you shouldn't care about them as people. I'm saying you should care more about your dream than what they think of you.

   You have to get over your fear of rejection. I bet you're grateful for other people who got over it. Think of all the hospitals, schools, programs, and non-profits that exist because people asked for money. And those people are no different from you. They were probably worried that they'd come across as annoying or greedy. But they believed enough in their vision to confront their fears and get over it. You must do the same.

6. *What if I lose Twitter followers?* Or Facebook friends? Or Instagram likes? This may sound insane to some of you, but it holds a lot of people back from asking for money. I don't have a lot to say about this, so I'll boil it down to one sentence: **Your friends don't want to hear about your dream forever, but they do want to hear about it for a season.**

7. *I don't have time.* Have you ever put together a piece of furniture the wrong way? After you lost your temper and said a few choice words, you finally decided to read the instructions for the first time. Once you saw the proper steps to assemble the piece you thought, *Ahhhhhh! Now, that makes a lot more sense! If only I*

had read the instructions the first time, I would've saved myself a lot of time.

Raising money is similar. Most people who don't do it right make it complicated. As a general rule, things that are more complicated take up more time. When you do it correctly—or simply—you'll be amazed at how much time it saves.

8. *I'm not being fully supported.* Every time you blame someone else, you absolve yourself of responsibility. That is the exact opposite of what I want you to do. I want you to see raising the money as *your* responsibility. So the lack of support from the school, the board, the parents, the students, the donors, your family, your friends, social media, your boss, etc.—it shouldn't ruin your day or your dreams. Why? Because it's not *their* responsibility, it's not *their* dream, it's yours.

Excuses, at the end of the day, are all based on one thing—fear. Fear of people. Fear of rejection. Fear of the unknown. Fear of failure. But that fear is based on emotion, not reality. Because of the way we've seen certain people raise money, we've convinced ourselves that it has to be as awkward as talking to your parents about sex. That simply isn't true. In this book, I want you to understand how to do it well (ask for money, that is—not talk to your parents about sex!). Your fears will still exist. And some of your excuses will be valid. But you have to move anyway. You have to do *something*. Or you will stay broke.

DON'T LET EXCUSES ROB YOUR VISION

The guy I mentioned at the beginning of this chapter . . . at the end of our lunch he looked at me and said, "Man, I feel like you just gave me a swift kick in the gut." Because I did. He was standing on a rug of excuses and I pulled it out from under him. All he could do was stand up, dust himself off, and get moving.

Don't quit! Don't put down this book. Read it, and then take action. I have a big step I want you to take at the end of this section. It's so simple, but your temptation will be to think of more excuses! Don't let excuses rob your vision. Your action will create the traction you need to get your dream on its feet!

CHAPTER 4

PEOPLE WILL NOT HATE YOU FOR ASKING FOR MONEY

One of the biggest barriers to funding your dreams is the fear that people will hate you if you ask for money.

Before we address that, let's take a minute and list the things that people actually hate:
1. Terrorists who are willing to murder innocent people.
2. Being punched in the face.
3. Snakes or spiders . . . maybe both.

Now for a few things I personally hate:
1. Auburn football.
2. Classical music.
3. Going to plays—of *any* kind.

If you love plays, don't get mad at me. If you love Auburn football, I don't care if you get mad at me. Just kidding. Kind of.

Notice that fundraisers are not on my list. They're probably not on yours, either. Think about it. You've been approached by football players selling coupon books for uniforms. Church kids selling donuts to raise money for camp. Cheerleaders selling candy bars to raise money for whatever it is cheerleaders raise money for. Did you hate them? No. You bought the donuts, ate half of them, and felt guilty about your calorie intake. Then you put your mind at ease by telling yourself that it was for a good cause. You didn't think: *Man, when that football player asked me to buy a coupon book, it made me hate football players . . . and I had never thought about hating them before.* No, you only hate football players if they pick on your son or date your daughter. You don't hate them if they ask you to buy a coupon book . . . that is intended to actually save you money.

Don't get me wrong, there are people out there who are annoying in their constant requests for handouts. But that's not you. If you're reading this book because you want a simple one-page plan to fund your dreams, you won't fall in the "annoying" category. And you certainly won't fall in the "I-hate-them" category.

The way you carry yourself when you ask for money will be a mirror to how people respond.

For instance:
- If you're nervous, it'll make them nervous.
- If you're awkward, it'll make them awkward.
- If you're scared, it'll make them scared.

On the other hand, this mirroring can work in your favor. If you're confident, it will give them confidence. If you're calm, they will feel calm. And if you approach each person with a gracious attitude, they will either give or decline graciously. On that note—and because I'm the king of cheesy phrases—I want you to remember something: **The proper attitude when raising money is gratitude.** You're welcome to make fun of it. But I sure hope it sticks in your brain.

Present your ask as an opportunity that people can partner with—as an opportunity for them to be a part of something that is going to make schools, communities, or the world a better place. The point isn't that people give you money. **The point is that you invite people to be a part of something that matters.** My pastor, Andy Stanley, says: "I don't want something *from* you. I want something *for* you." That should be your stance when you raise money.

I do this when I represent my own company. I blatantly ask people to buy our resources because in my heart, I honestly believe our products

STEP ONE: OWN IT

will help them. It's not just a sale to me, it's an invitation for our clients to take a step in a better direction. When I see that what we offer intersects with someone's needs, I get fired up. It makes me excited to ask. When you can come to this point in your heart, that's when you'll notice a shift in your success.

I have a friend named Carey who's the pastor of a large church in Canada, eh. Carey is a very sharp guy. I've learned a lot from him about everything from leadership to business to parenting. Carey's church was a million dollar organization at one point. But they had no margin. They had some money in the bank, but they couldn't gain any forward progress. Carey called me and asked if I would help him figure out why they were stuck.

I listened to a bunch of Carey's sermons. He did a phenomenal job of informing his audience of the church's financial needs. He even did a great job of creating inspiration and emotion around why people give. But one thing I noticed was that Carey never came right out and *asked* people to give. And I knew why. It was uncomfortable to him. He didn't want people to think he was greedy or aggressive. But when Carey realized that his church was suffering financially because he wasn't clearly and deliberately asking for money, he immediately shifted his position.

Here's what Carey decided: "This is *my* responsibility. I'm going to own this. Until this church creates a little breathing room, I'm not going to stop asking for money." Then he took it one step further and decided that he didn't just want his *church* to have more financial margin, but he also wanted its *individuals* to have it. So, he planned a series of messages around the topic of financial stewardship. Then, he invited 300 families to take part in making their church, and their lives, healthier.

> YOU'LL SEE PEOPLE THROUGH THE OPPORTUNITY LENS, NOT THE OBSTACLE LENS

In one year, the giving in his church increased by twenty-two percent. They now operate with a couple years worth of reserves. They are fully funded. But more than that, the people who gave bettered themselves in the process.

Carey shifted his attitude. He stopped viewing asking people as an obstacle, and he started viewing *inviting* them as an opportunity.

When you change, like Carey did, everything else will change, too.

You'll see people through the opportunity lens, not the obstacle lens. Asking people for money will become a pleasure instead of a worry. Because you'll know that you're offering people a chance to be a part of something that makes a difference.

It's time for you to own it! It's time for you to start your one-page plan. And it's time for you to take your first step toward funding your dream.

So, get your pen out and get ready to own it!

(YOUR NAME) IS RESPONSIBLE FOR RAISING THE FUNDS.

SECTION II

THE ONE-PAGE PLAN
STEP TWO: CLARIFY IT

CHAPTER 5

CLARITY CREATES CERTAINTY, AND CERTAIN PEOPLE TAKE MASSIVE ACTION

I meet with people all the time who tell me they need to raise some money. I ask them how much. They shrug. At that point, I realize they're trying to grab a vapor. They're reaching for a reality that doesn't exist yet.

In order to fund your dream, you need to clarify your plan. I'm not talking about an intimidating plan. I'm talking about a simple, one-two process:
1. Pick a dollar amount you want to raise.
2. Pick a date you want to raise it by.

> CLARIFYING YOUR PLAN = FUNDING YOUR DREAM.

Just like that, people will go from taking no steps to taking big steps. That's why this step in *The One-Page Plan* is such a big deal. Because when it comes to raising money, clarity creates certainty, and certain people take massive action.

Another thing clarity does is serve as a magnet between you and your goal. Clarity will pull you through tough times. It's the anchor you can grab when you feel like you're going under. If you say you're going to raise 30 grand in 30 days—and you start to feel anxious—you can look at your date, look at your dollar amount, and then take the next right step in that direction.

My wife and I said we wanted to be completely debt-free by the time we were 30. I'm not sure why we said that. Maybe we lost our minds. But knowing *what* we wanted—and *when* we wanted it by—influenced every dime we spent (or, more specifically, *didn't* spend). That *what* and *when* pushed and pulled us through.

You've got to clarify your future. Complexity and mystification kill action. **When you say, "sometime soon," it really means, "nowhere fast."**

Back to my wife. When she and I were dating in college, I knew that I loved her. But I was wrestling with the idea of telling her. I was nervous because I didn't know what she'd say in return. But one day I decided, "It's time." I don't know what was so special about that particular day, but I woke up and made the decision that today would be the day I would tell Kacie, "I love you." I immediately started sweating. To calm my nerves, I put a Smashing Pumpkins CD in (remember CD players?) and played "Tonight, Tonight" on repeat. The goal was *very* clear. My mind was made up. It was happening tonight . . . actually, it was happening "Tonight, Tonight."

On our drive back to campus after our date, I knew it was time. I thought back to the commitment I made to myself earlier that day. I couldn't back out now. I can still picture it vividly in my mind. Red light. I counted down from 10 to 1 at least three times. Then I blurted out, "Kacie, I love you!"

Victory! I was so fired up. I did it! I set a clear goal and made myself follow through with it.

Kacie, on the other hand—not so fired up. She said nothing. That's right . . . total silence.

I later realized that blurting at a stoplight wasn't the most romantic way to say "I love you" to a girl for the first time. But that's not the point (at least, not in *this* book). The point is, I made a commitment to myself, and that commitment pushed me past my fear and anxiety. It propelled me toward my goal.

STEP TWO: CLARIFY IT

And a couple of years later—for reasons I'll never understand—that same girl agreed to marry me. I'm not sure if it was *because* of my stoplight declaration, or in spite of it.

Here's what I've learned: **you can be uncertain about outcomes, but you can't be unclear about them.** Think about people who go off to war. They're never convinced of the outcome. But you better believe there's a clear plan in place.

You see, without taking this step, you can't move forward. You're just floating around in the dream world of *I hope, I wish,* and *sometime.*

Two important things about clarity:

1. *You* need it. Clarity will help you stay grounded in the present. It allows you to measure your progress. You will feel motivated to push harder because you have a solid understanding of where you are and how far you have to go.

2. *Donors* need it. Clarity gives donors perspective. And it drives them to make a decision because they feel a sense of urgency around a deadline.

Let me give you an example. I told you about my wife and I going to my daughter's kindergarten open house. The PTA had fundraising tables set up. I'll say this again: thank God for the PTA. That crew gets a lot of stuff done. But in this particular instance, the people sitting behind the tables were doing just that—sitting behind tables.

I think there was a sign on the table that said *Make Kids' Futures Brighter* or something like that. But there was no specific information. My wife asked them what they were raising money for. They handed her a sheet of paper that was general and vague. There was no deadline on when the money needed to be raised.

I'm sure the people behind the table were incredible. And I'm confident they were doing the best they could. But my wife and I couldn't have been more underwhelmed. We certainly weren't inspired to give. But because we had struck up a conversation—and we were standing right in front of them—we felt obligated to give *something*.

This is important to know: a check written out of obligation is always smaller than a check written out of excitement.

Recently, I was standing in line at Smoothie King. If you've never had their Gladiator Smoothie, you should try it. It's a protein shake, and for some reason it makes you feel like your muscles are bigger. Trust me, I need all the help I can get! While I was there, a student approached me and said he was raising money for his high school football team. He explained that he had a coupon card that would save me money on the smoothie I was about to buy. Then he said, "I have to sell 20 of these cards by the end of the week. Would you like to buy one?" Of course I would.

This student used a date and a dollar amount to drive me—a potential donor—to give. I knew what I was contributing to. And I knew why and when. I bet he sold all 20 cards in one day.

One reason people don't do this is because they don't have clear goals in their own lives. I define goal setting as *deciding what you want and writing it down.* I have a mentor I admire from afar named Jim Rohm. He says that only three percent of people actually write down their goals. It's a lot easier to say, "I'm going to lose some weight," than it is to say, "I'm going to lose 10 pounds in one month." Because, then we have accountability. It anchors our commitment. That's why, at the end of this section, you'll have an opportunity to anchor *your* commitment.

Another reason people struggle with this is they're afraid to get it wrong. They think, *What if I fail at hitting my dollar amount by the date I set?* First, I don't set goals that are next-to-impossible. I set goals that stretch me. A goal to lose 10 pounds in a month makes a lot more sense than a goal to lose 50 pounds in a month. But losing 10 pounds isn't easy, either (I know that firsthand). Secondly, you're not always going to hit the mark. Even though Kacie and I were fully committed to being debt-free by 30, we didn't hit our mark. But we did when we were 31. If we had never written that goal down, we'd still be in debt today. Because it drove and pushed us to keep working toward our objective, even though we didn't meet our initial deadline.

This step in *The One-Page Plan* comes with a number of benefits. For starters, **you gain confidence.** If you were about to jump off a cliff and knew that a net would catch you at the bottom, that would be encouraging, right? Grant it, at the end of the day you're still jumping off a cliff, so you're probably not going to be too encouraged. But it's certainly a lot better than jumping off a cliff and hoping a net will

STEP TWO: CLARIFY IT

catch you at the bottom. When it comes to raising money, knowing exactly what you need and when you need it by creates stability, a net. It's assuring. Without it, you're jumping off a fundraising cliff with no certainty about what's going to happen next.

Another benefit of clarity is that **you reduce stress.** I know people who've been raising money their entire professional lives. They never rest. They're always tense and anxious. Why? Because they don't have a date and dollar amount clarified. They live in a constant state of "I need to raise more money." Listen, even if it's your job to constantly raise money, you still need deadlines. You still need some quarterly or bi-annual date and dollar amounts that allow you to track and measure your progress.

Finally, **you increase generosity.** If you're unclear, people won't give as much. My wife and I gave some money to the PTA table. But I'm confident that we would've written a bigger check if the people at that table would've explained their plan and purpose. Clarity prompts people to give more.

When I meet with businesses ,I ask them to write down their top three objectives for their company. Almost ninety-nine percent percent of the time, none of their goals line up. Everybody just assumes they're on the same page. But because they've never clarified their objectives, they're not. So, I help them move toward clarity. Because when people get clear, they get going. They move. Just like a runner who sees the finish line. They reach their goals and ultimately fund their dreams.

That's what I want to do in this section—get you going. Take the next step in your one-page plan. It's time to move!

CHAPTER 6

HOW MUCH MONEY DO YOU NEED AND BY WHEN?

You would think that when people set out to fund their dreams, these two questions would be the first things they answer. But as I've stated, I've worked with businesses, non-profits, churches, and every other sector out there, and I've learned that people simply don't know. Either the goal isn't clear, or they haven't taken the time to establish it. But somehow they skip this step.

You can't skip it!

Listen, **when you choose a date and dollar amount, the success rate of your fundraiser grows exponentially.** On the other hand, when you mystify it—you settle for an unidentified dream and a general amount of money—you limit yourself. People simply won't give as much. Why? Because people want clarity. They want the target to be clear and concise.

So, pick a date!

Dates are huge. I don't know about you, but I'm bad about avoiding decisions until I have to make them. Applications. Work deadlines. Oil changes. I put things off until I know I can't put them off anymore. You may be like me in that regard. That sense of urgency, however, can work in your favor when it comes to raising money.

Have you ever noticed that people get more interested in sporting events when it gets closer to the end of the game? Some of my friends don't even bother watching football games until the fourth quarter. Not me. I tune into a University of Alabama game about six hours *before* kickoff. But the not-so-committed fans get involved as the game progresses (and yes, I do heckle them about how their complacency is hurting our program!).

When you take this step and tell people a deadline, you're sparking interest. You're tuning them in. You're letting them know when the fourth quarter ends. You're driving them to make decisions.

When you pick a date, it communicates a sense of urgency to your donors. Professional fundraisers, this goes for you, too (by the way, thank you for reading this book! I'm honored). Decide the deadlines ahead of time. Will they occur every week? Every month? You choose the length of the game. Then convey that information to your donors. When you hit that date, communicate the next one. Donors react to deadlines (more about that later in this book).

Now that you have a date in mind, the next step is to pick a dollar amount.

When you specify a dollar amount, it tells potential donors that you have a plan. And it gives them context for how their contribution fits into that plan. For instance, $100 toward a goal of $1,000 feels a lot more significant to donors than $100 toward a goal of $100,000.

I've met with a lot of people who launch into raising money and pick an amount out of thin air. They'll say they need to raise $75,000. I'll ask, "Are you sure you need *that much?*" Or, "Are you sure you need that much r*ight now?*" If so, I'll encourage them to break up the amounts: X *amount* for start-up money, X *amount* for advertising, etc. To me, fundraising installments are better than one lump sum.

Do your research before you announce your financial need. When potential donors ask you why you need $45,000 in 30 days, be able to

STEP TWO: CLARIFY IT

clearly explain it. Donors respond to specifics. You need clarity and a plan.

In 2012, Oklahoma was devastated by tornadoes. I got home from work that day and felt sick over the news. Hundreds were killed, and thousands were left homeless. Some of those families had kids that were the same age as mine. I couldn't sleep that night. And the next day I couldn't stop thinking about it.

So, I acted. Within 24 hours, a team of us had a website up that clearly stated our fundraising goal:

> *In seven days, we want to raise $15,000 to give to the victims of the Oklahoma tornadoes.*

Our website was featured on NBC, Huffington Post, and a ton of other sites.

But we didn't get caught up in the hype. We stuck with our one-page plan. We kept the date and dollar amount in front of everyone's eyes. We said over and over, "We need $15,000 in seven days. And we want it to go *directly* to these families in need." We had a date. We had a dollar amount. And in seven days, we raised $50,000.

I don't tell you that because I want to be the hero of this story (I'm saving that for my memoir). I wasn't seeking any notoriety. There were people on my team that did way more—and raised way more—than I did. Nobody in Oklahoma City even knew my name. No, the hero of this story is the amount of money that we raised. And that should be the hero of your fundraising story, too. Why? *Because the actual amount is the actual money that is actually used to help actual people.*

Most people feel timid when it comes to raising money. They're afraid to say exactly how much they need. And that creates a huge obstacle. Because when you're timid and hesitant, you'll almost always talk *around* the goal. You'll be unclear. You'll sound unprepared. And unfortunately, **a lack of clarity will kill your fundraiser faster than anything else.**

So, how much money do you need? And when do you need it by?
If everyone in your company, family, team, and group of friends doesn't know the answer to these questions, you're in trouble. And trust me,

the last thing I want for you is to be in trouble. I want you to succeed! That's why I overemphasize this point. And that's why I want you to take a big step at the end of this section.

PICK A DATE AND DOLLAR AMOUNT, DANG IT!

Most people—myself included—read a book and do *nothing* when the author challenges them to act.

This is not that book.

What I need you to do right now is to stop thinking about this in the abstract. In fact, stop thinking about it *too much*. Just pick how much you need and the date by which you need it.

If you can't take that step right now, you need to work through it quickly. Get over your fears, and pick a date and dollar amount, dang it.

Pick it and stick with it!

CHAPTER 7

TELL THE WORLD HOW MUCH MONEY YOU WILL RAISE AND BY WHEN

After you pick a date and dollar amount, one of the best things you can do is go public with the information. Send it out to everyone you know. Put it on Facebook and Instagram. Text and email your friends. Do whatever you can to let people know your goal.

I've seen a lot of people pick a date and dollar amount and then stop there. They stall. No more forward progress. Maybe they're unsure of what to do next. I personally don't think it needs to be complicated. Pick a date and dollar amount, write it down, and then broadcast it to the world.

When we created the website to raise money for Oklahoma City, I immediately went to my social media outlets. I posted that I was going to raise $15,000 in seven days. I got instant buy-in from some of my friends. I'm sure there were others who thought I was being arrogant or self-promoting. I don't let stuff like that slow me down. All I was doing was revealing my intentions. And when I revealed them to the people within my circle of influence, it pot-committed me to the cause I wanted to support.

After you pick a date and dollar amount, one of the best things you can do is go public with the information. Send it out to everyone you know. Put it on Facebook and Instagram. Text and email your friends. Do whatever you can to let people know your goal.

I've seen a lot of people pick a date and dollar amount and then stop there. They stall. No more forward progress. Maybe they're unsure of what to do next. I personally don't think it needs to be complicated. Pick a date and dollar amount, write it down, and then broadcast it to the world.

When we created the website to raise money for Oklahoma City, I immediately went to my social media outlets. I posted that I was going to raise $15,000 in seven days. I got instant buy-in from some of my friends. I'm sure there were others who thought I was being arrogant or self-promoting. I don't let stuff like that slow me down. All I was doing was revealing my intentions. And when I revealed them to the people within my circle of influence, it pot-committed me to the cause I wanted to support.

If you're wondering what "pot-committed" means, by the way, I'll explain it. According to UrbanDictionary.com, *pot-committed* means,

GOING PUBLIC > ONLY TELLING YOUR SPOUSE

"The act of having put in so many chips, or otherwise risk of consequence, that you might as well follow through with the plan." Which brings me to this important question: where would I be in life without Urban Dictionary? It interprets song lyrics for me. It gives me cool gambling terms to use in my book. What a resource!

I took a personality profile called the StrengthsFinder test and discovered that *Responsibility* is one of my top three strengths. It doesn't mean I adopt stray cats, by the way. I've never actually had a stray cat wander onto my property. I'm not sure what I would do. If you're an animal lover, just know that I wouldn't do anything cruel. Anyway, my *Responsibility* strength means I'm intrinsically tied to doing something if I say I will. So, when I announce to people that I'm going to raise a certain amount of money within a certain amount of time, I feel accountable for it.

Even if you're convinced you'd score low in the responsibility category, you still feel the pressure and urgency when people are watching and

STEP TWO: CLARIFY IT

waiting to see if you'll follow through. That's why, when it comes to sharing your goal for raising money:

All of a sudden, you have a ticking time bomb in your hands. You are motivated and hungry. Guess what? So are the people watching you. They want to know how this whole thing will turn out. And if you care at all about your credibility, you will work hard—come hell or high water—to reach your goals. *That* is accountability at its finest!

Whatever you write down for your date and dollar amount, I want you to announce it. Right now. Stop reading. I'm serious, get on Instagram, Twitter, Tumblr, or whatever social media outlet you like, and tell the world your goal. Text your mama. Email your grandma (if your grandma is email-savvy) and say: "Meemaw, I'm gonna raise $_____ in the next _____ days. Just wanted to let you know."

Let me ask you a simple question: Are you all in? If so, take the next step in *The One-Page Plan*. Don't overanalyze it. Don't second-guess it. Just put it out there. Show everyone (including yourself) that you're serious about your fundraising goals.

I WILL RAISE
$ _____

BY
___/ ___/ 20___

SECTION III

THE ONE-PAGE PLAN
STEP THREE: PLAN IT

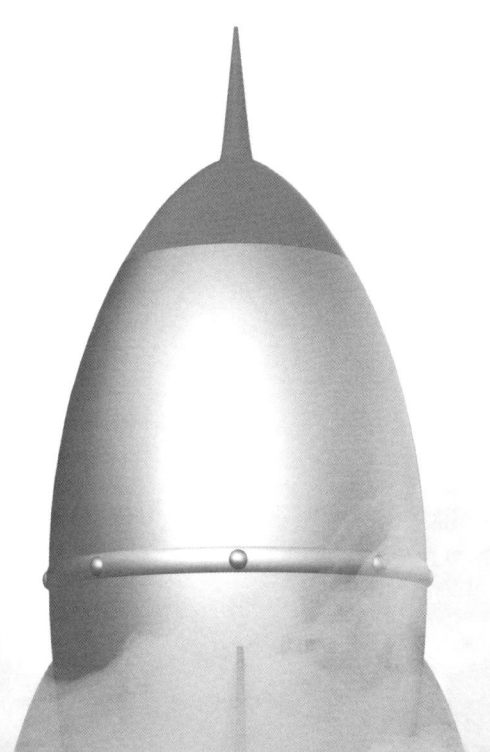

CHAPTER 8

PASSION IS BETTER WITH A PLAN

A couple years ago, I was hanging out at my house on a Sunday evening. And I vividly remember looking at myself in the mirror and thinking, Gosh, I look rough! I didn't just look rough, I *felt* rough. To be honest, I was disgusted with my health. I ate terribly, drank soda all the time, and never exercised. So, I vowed to change my life the very next day.

So, there I was . . . Monday morning. Standing in the gym. Wearing a plain white tee and a pair of 20-year-old gym shorts. I had *nothing* in terms of a game plan, so I simply went down the line and attempted every machine in the building. I even did the machine where you sit down and push the weights out until your legs are spread. A human body is *not* designed to feel that type of pain (and it's really awkward to use that machine with other people around). I even ran on the treadmill. And in the middle of my torturous workout, I vowed to *completely* change my diet. Cut out all the junk food.

My new fitness plan lasted a total of six days.

Two weeks later, I was sitting at my favorite local restaurant, Roosters, stuffing my face with hot wings. Extra hot sauce. Extra blue cheese on the side. Later that night, I ordered pizza and had it delivered to my house. This is not an exaggeration: I sat in the living room and ate a post-dinner pizza by *myself!* I felt like I couldn't get full no matter how much I ate.

The next morning, I found myself in front of the mirror again. You can imagine how that conversation went. I kept throwing words like *failure, miserable,* and *weak* at myself.

But that experience taught me something: **Passion gets me going, but it doesn't keep me going.** The same is true when it comes to raising money. You may feel passionate about your cause. But that passion will only take you so far. It can ignite a spark. It can inspire motivation. But if you want to sustain your drive, you need a plan.

PASSION WITHOUT A PLAN BRINGS PAIN

The reason most people don't create a plan when they raise money is impatience. They get distracted by things like urgency, excitement, and fear. But you can't afford not to plan. Abraham Lincoln once said, "Give me six hours to chop down a tree, and I'll spend the first four sharpening my axe." There's a reason why President Lincoln's face is on money. He knew how to make it, keep it, and multiply it.

Passion without a plan brings pain. On the other hand, if you plug your passion into a system, you can go places quickly and successfully.

So, let's create a plan! Start by answering these five questions:

1. **What are you selling?** It's important that you learn how to craft your story. Because although you're raising money, you're still selling something. People have to believe in your idea or business before they write you a check.
2. **When are you selling it?** Create a calendar for your fundraiser. Picking dates and setting up deadlines is huge.
3. **Who will help you sell it?** *You* have to own the outcome. But you should certainly surround yourself with as many supportive players as you need. Core team members will help you get the job done effectively.
4. **How will you communicate to donors?** If you communicate the same message the same way to everybody, you make them feel like a nobody. Your messages—and the ways in which they're communicated—should feel tailored and personal.

STEP THREE: PLAN IT

5. **How will you receive donations?** The easier the payment method, the more people are going to give. You *have* to make this simple.

Don't get nervous or panic. We'll walk through each one of these in this section. Remember, you can fit the whole plan onto one page!

I have the same ritual every time I fly. I'll take you through it step by step:

1. I buy a bag of Twizzlers® candy and a bottle of Perrier® Sparkling Water on the way to the airport.
2. I board the plane.
3. I eat the bag of Twizzlers and drink the bottle of Perrier before the plane takes off.
4. I go to sleep until the plane elevates to 30,000 feet.
5. I wake up when the "free-to-walk-about-the-cabin" bell rings.
6. I climb over the person next to me and make a stop at the bathroom.
7. I climb back over my neighbor to sit down, ensuring that he or she hates me forever.
8. I open my computer and put my headphones on.
9. I put an Imagine Dragons album on repeat until the plan lands.

Obviously, I've flown a *lot*.

I've flown on planes of every size. From those tiny six-seaters that make you convinced you're going to die at any moment, to those jumbo jets with two stories and beds that lay flat. Here's something I've learned about flying: **the larger the plane, the longer the runway needs to be.**

That's how it works with raising money, too. The more money you want to raise, the more groundwork you need to lay before you begin. Don't get impatient. And don't believe the lie that passion alone will take you where you want to go. If you take the time to put a solid plan in place, your fundraiser will take off.

I'll help you take the next step and create your runway at the end of this section. Trust me on this: *The One-Page Plan* will get your plane soaring!

CHAPTER 9

INGREDIENT ONE: A COMPELLING STORY

My favorite movie of all time is *National Lampoon's Christmas Vacation*. You might not think it's funny. But I think you're wrong. Come on . . . Cousin Eddie? The cat getting electrocuted by the Christmas tree? Clark's holiday "bonus" to the Jelly-of-the-Month club? What's not to love? It's about family, pressure at work, conflict, holiday expectations . . . so many things people can relate to.

Everyone likes a good story. That's why people watch television, go to the movies, and read books. And you can't raise money successfully without one.

To create the story for your fundraiser, start by answering this question: what are you *selling?* I introduced this question in the last chapter, so you should've already started thinking about it. Is it an idea? A cause? Aid? Research? Education? If you're raising money, you're asking people to give in exchange for *something.* You have to define what that "something" is.

There are three components to a great fundraising story:

1. **Short.** Keep your story short and sweet. If you can't tweet it, put it in a Facebook post, or send it in a quick text, your story is too long. We live in a low-attention span world. If you have to drone on and on for people to "get it," you need a new story. If you have to explain yourself over and over again, you need a better hook.

2. **Simple.** Don't make the story complicated. Use common language that everyone can understand. So many people cloud their story with strange or overly sophisticated language. Avoid this at all costs. If your grandma and plumber don't understand what you're raising money for, start over. Stick to the facts, and present them in a way that makes sense to anyone.

3. **Selfless.** The best stories ensure that you are *not* the focal point. The focus might be the idea, the benefit, the donor, or the cause. But take yourself out of the story as much as possible. Don't make *yourself* the hero.

My friend, Michael, has a daughter who wanted to write a book called *The Clown Who Lost His Funny*. Great title, huh? I should've used that title for this book, with a picture of me giving two thumbs up on the cover.

Michael wanted to help his daughter get funding for her book. So, he asked people to give money. Here's what he said: "Please help my 12-year-old daughter write a book." And that was it. Michael kept it brilliantly short and simple. He didn't use vague or sappy language. He simply stated what the money was for. Notice that he also didn't say, "Help me raise money for my daughter." He put her at the forefront— she was the beneficiary. Any time you can involve and highlight a kid in your story, it benefits your campaign.

Michael's daughter surpassed her $5,500 goal, and her book will be published soon.

Another example of a great fundraising story is from my friend, Philip. Philip is a ridiculously talented photographer. As his photography business grew, he saved up a lot of money and bought himself a vintage motorcycle. Before he even had a chance to get his bike insured, it was stolen. Gone. Taken.

So, he started a campaign called Let Phil Ride. He asked people to give

STEP THREE: PLAN IT

money so he could purchase another motorcycle. At first, this sounds like a completely selfish ask. But Phil didn't make himself the main beneficiary. He created a website called LetPhilRide.com where people could purchase discount photography sessions from his business. My wife and I bought one. Every penny went to replace his stolen bike. Philip created a donor benefit to his fundraiser. If you gave to his campaign, the hero of the story was the new family photographs. Philip had a new bike within a couple of weeks.

WHAT'S YOUR STORY?

You need a story. And there's no better time to write it than now. Make sure you keep it *short, simple*, and *selfless*. That will help you create a sticky story that people can't get away from until they give. You'll have a chance to plug it into your one-page plan at the end of this section.

CHAPTER 10

INGREDIENT TWO: A CONCRETE CALENDAR

Let me ask you a question. Do you want to raise a small amount of money slowly or a large amount of money quickly? Stupid question, right? It's like one of those questions a college professor asks at the beginning of his first lecture to get you to pay attention in his class all semester—something like, "Do you want to succeed when you leave this university?" You think, *No, I want to be an idiot and fail your course.* Then he tells you that you have to show up at every single class and take notes during his boring lectures.

Of course you want to raise a lot of money! And sure, you'd love to do it fast. But I've seen a lot of fundraising techniques that seem to point toward slow, low-bearing results. The successful plans for raising money, however, always point toward creating a calendar. Why? Because a calendar will set you up and propel you to raise a lot of money quickly. And I hope *that* interests you enough to pay attention for the rest of this class.

The reason a calendar makes such a difference is it creates comfort for you and your donors. It creates the parameters for you to take inventory of the things you need, and it sets the pace for your fundraiser. A calendar also reduces stress. It breaks seemingly overwhelming tasks into manageable chunks. It helps you to spread out your passion over time, preventing you from burning out or giving up.

One of the most important things I've ever learned about raising money is that it's most effective when it's presented as a campaign. I'm not talking about "campaigning" at a presidential-election level. That's too long a process. I'm talking about a clearly defined season of time designated for you to raise money. You create the start date and finish date. Like we talked about in the last section, you create the beginning and end of the game. The first and fourth quarter. The kickoff and the final whistle. The dial and the hang-up. Okay, you get the idea.

Otherwise, you will be perpetually striving. And sadly, that almost always fails.

Even if you're in charge of raising operational expenses, salaries, or long-term financial needs, you still need to break it up into campaigns. Here's why: without a campaign, you just come off as someone who constantly asks for money. You don't want to be that person. So, create a calendar for raising money.

People understand campaigns. They know that campaigns have start and end dates, so eventually the asking-for-money will stop (as opposed to perpetual fundraising, where the asking has no end).

Campaigns represent focused energy. My buddy, Michael, calls it "forced and focused labor." Think of it this way. The sun represents a ton of energy. When we stand beneath the sun, however, we don't go up in flames. That's because the sun's energy is spread out over hundreds of thousands of miles. But think about what happens when you take a magnifying glass and concentrate that same energy on an ant. It catches on fire (I'm sorry, animal lovers). Why? Because you've taken the sun's energy and forced it in one direction. That's what campaigns do—set ants on fire. Just kidding. They take a large amount of potential energy and channel it to a particular focus.

Now is the time to put your one-page plan into overdrive. There is a lot you could do. But you need to take the steps to get your plan *focused*. Choose the start and end date to your campaign. Create a calendar. This will help you. It will help your donors. And it will help your campaign.

STEP THREE: PLAN IT

To successfully execute a campaign, it must have three phases.

PHASE ONE: BEFORE THE ASK

Most people want to start raising money immediately. But you shouldn't. Before you try to land the plane of raising money, you must prepare the runway. I like the way that sounds, so I'm going to say it again: *Before you try to land the plane of raising money, you must prepare the runway.* Writing out your one-page plan is part of that preparation. So is networking, gathering contact info, and writing out all your communication: pre-draft letters, tweets, emails, texts, etc. Have them lined up before the official ask. If you're going to utilize design and technology (logos, websites, etc.), this is the time to get that stuff figured out.

There is a lot of random, busywork that comes with raising money. Do that before the big ask. **Because once you launch your campaign, the donors should be your solitary focus.**

One thing I always do is what I call the *Drip Before You Drop* method. No, it has nothing to do with bathroom etiquette. I believe in "dripping" your vision in strategic places before "dropping" a full-throttle campaign. I'll send a few tweets, texts, or emails. Something like, "Hey, next Monday I'm going to start a seven-day campaign to raise money for cancer patients. Stay tuned for details!" This alerts people to the fact that a campaign is coming, it will have an end-date, they will get more information soon, and I will possibly ask them to contribute.

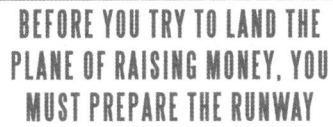
BEFORE YOU TRY TO LAND THE PLANE OF RAISING MONEY, YOU MUST PREPARE THE RUNWAY

PHASE TWO: THE ASK

Once you've prepared your runway, your vision is ready to land. Since you've dripped before dropping, people won't be caught off guard by your ask. And people know your ask has an ending point (also strange). Now people are ready to hear from you.

Within the specified time of your campaign, I want you to create small goals. One goal per day is a great start. For example, "I want to raise $100 by the end of day one." Or, "By day two, we want to get to $300." Or both. Little goals will push you along. Put pressure on yourself—do whatever it takes—to reach those small goals. Before you know it, your campaign will be over and you will have reached your big goal!

PHASE THREE: AFTER THE ASK

Don't go home yet. Your job isn't over. In phase three, you need to park the plane at the terminal gate and take care of your passengers. This is where you send thank-you notes. This is when you update your donors on the outcome of the fundraiser. This is when you follow through with people who mentioned giving, but didn't. **You have to treat these people well—not just because you might want them to give again one day, but because it's the right thing to do.** Out of all three steps, this one may be the most important.

I realize that there's a wide range of things you could be raising money for. That's why we've put several sample checklists for your calendar on our website. Go to **FundraisingRocket.com/tools** and find the calendar that fits your goal and meets your needs.

Benjamin Franklin once said, "By failing to prepare, you are preparing to fail." There may be no arena of life where that quote is more appropriate than the field of raising money. But you can prevent failure by following *The One-Page Plan*.

CHAPTER 11

INGREDIENT THREE: AN ON-BOARD TEAM

This past weekend my wife and I met four of our friends for dinner at our favorite Cuban restaurant. We stayed for hours. It was so much fun. It all started with a conga line. It ended with my friend Ben twerking while I rapped "Ice Ice Baby" on stage with the band. If you don't know what "twerking" is, well, I don't know what to tell you. You can check UrbanDictionary.com for a colorful definition . . . honestly, I wouldn't worry about it.

We left the restaurant and loaded in my wife's minivan (yeah, we're cool like that!). We wanted to keep the party rolling. So, what did we do? We collectively decided to roll someone's yard. We're in our 30s. We all have multiple kids. No club hopping or barhopping for us. We have to create our mischief and still be back in time to get our kids from the babysitter.

It was my wife's idea. Isn't she awesome? In moments like that, it's obvious why we're meant for each other. She owned the outcome. She drove us to Kroger to buy toilet paper. Then she dropped us off a block away from our target house. While she stayed back as our getaway driver, the rest of us piled out of the van and crept toward the house. It was time to go to work!

Holly is almost 30 years old (the only one in our crew who's pre-30). She had never rolled a house before. She walked right up to the front window and started covering the front hedges. I'm not sure if she's brave or dumb. Her husband, Ben, is the same height as a giraffe. He stood at the edge of the yard and hurled rolls of toilet paper as high as he could into the trees. My buddy, Louie, helped me take care of the lower branches. His wife Lindsay played lookout, which turned out to be a much-needed job, because there was a suspicious car on the prowl.

Once we ran out of toilet paper, we sprinted back to our getaway minivan. Ben wiped out on the neighbor's lawn. Little did we know, he lost his cell phone in the tumble. We were two miles down the road when he said, "Guys, we have a problem." So, we had to turn around and sneak back onto the premises. Talk about a bunch of amateurs!

It was a night I'll never forget. And it's a silly example, but the reason I had so much fun is because of the teamwork that went into that experience. I could've rolled that yard by myself. And I suppose I could've done a decent job. But it wouldn't have been as fast, effective, or fun. And honestly, it would've been a little bit weird—a random guy rolling a yard by himself. Having good teammates makes all the difference.

Teamwork functions the same way when it comes to raising money (yes, I just compared fundraising to rolling someone's yard). You need to have a hand-selected team of three to five people who will help you meet your goals. I still believe you should own the outcome. *You* should manage the process. But that doesn't mean you don't need help along the way. Here's why:

1. **If you don't have a team, you'll quit.** Fundraising is hard. You need people to encourage you and remind you why you're doing what you're doing.
2. **A team helps you go further faster.** Four people carrying a couch works a lot better than one.
3. **It's more fun with a team.** Like I said, we had a blast rolling that yard the other night. But what made it fun was that we did it *together*. Working with a team provides an enriching dynamic that makes the process enjoyable.
4. **A team compensates for your weaknesses.** Different people have different skills. Are you a bad writer? Find a good one, and put him or her on your team. A team helps you boost the total package that you present to the world.

STEP THREE: PLAN IT

Any time I've been successful at raising money, it wasn't because of me. On my own, I'm just a country boy from Birmingham. I don't put on successful fundraisers by myself. I can't. No, everything is made possible through a team.

Here's what I do when it's time to recruit core team members. **First, I ask people to make a specific time commitment.** For instance, I'll say, "Will you please be involved before, during, and after this fundraiser?" That way, they know up front what kind of time commitment I'm asking for. **Second, I focus on the desired outcome.** I do that by saying things like, "Tyler, will you please help me raise money for orphans in Haiti?" I try to communicate to potential team members the same way I communicate to donors—with focused clarity. **Third, I give them a specific task.** "Will you build the website and manage all the technology needs for this fundraiser?" "Will you do all the written communication?" "Will you meet 10 people for coffee and tell them what we're raising money for?"

Define your fundraising strengths before you build your team. I'm good at directly asking people for money and building a team. That means I always need help with technology and administrative details. One thing I always try to do is get a celebrity spokesperson. I ask him or her to promote—and publicly align themselves with—my need. I'm not saying you need Justin Timberlake to successfully raise money (although if you can get him, go for it!). I'm talking about anyone who is well known within a certain industry, community, or group. I also send messages to people in the social media world who can create an online buzz about my fundraiser. I pay some of them. Others I ask to volunteer. But I make sure everyone believes in the ultimate vision behind the smaller tasks and goals.

> **DEFINE YOUR FUNDRAISING STRENGTH BEFORE YOU BUILD YOUR TEAM**

Look, if you can't get a few people to commit to helping your cause, you probably won't be able to get a lot of people to commit to giving to your cause. But if you can add this ingredient, an on-board team, to your one-page plan, you might find yourself *exactly* where you want to be in a short amount of time.

And you'll have a lot more fun getting there!

CHAPTER 12

INGREDIENT FOUR: A TARGETED AUDIENCE

When is the last time you thought, *Man, I really want to be treated like a nobody?* Exactly. No one ever thinks that. There are probably times when you wish you were *invisible* . . . like when you're passing a mall kiosk and you get spotted by a commission-based calendar salesman. But you never want to be treated like a nobody. But that's what old-school fundraising does—it treats everybody equally. It's a nice thought, but everybody doesn't want to feel like *everybody*—they want to feel like *somebody*. I see it all the time on social media. People post things like, "If everybody who sees this gives $100, we can reach our goals and impact this cause." That's an ineffective post. If everybody is "everybody," nobody is somebody.

Donors are human beings. They come from a wide variety of backgrounds and experiences. To do one general, blanket ask devalues individuals and alienates them. Think about it: you approach different people in different ways in normal conversation. Doesn't it make sense that you would do that same thing in fundraising?

It starts by creating a targeted message. Let's talk about how to do that.

Start by drawing three circles. **In the middle circle, put the names of**

people with whom you have significant relational equity. My friend Van Baird taught me that term. If you have *relational equity* with people, it means you have poured into, developed, or made meaningful relational deposits with them. And now that you're raising money, you may want to make a withdrawal in return. These are the people you love, who love you, and who you immediately think of when you ask yourself, *Who is the most likely to support me and my cause?* You shouldn't send these people a copy of a mass-email or support letter. You should take them out to dinner or coffee. **Ask them one-on-one.** If you can't meet face to face, send them a text (an individual text, not a mass text). Or, call them on the phone. Or Skype them. Or Facetime them. Or use some new technology that was invented after this book was written.

In addition to people you have relational equity with, **also put people in this circle who have significant financial margin.** These are the people who can write bigger checks. They're not more important than everyone else. But you do need to treat them differently than everyone else.

Recently, my wife and I went to Nashville to see my favorite band. Want to know who my favorite band is? No? You don't? Too bad, I'm going to tell you anyway. They're called Imagine Dragons, and they're awesome. I was so excited.

As luck would have it, we randomly met their tour manager in our hotel lobby. We struck up a conversation with her (I acted like a 12-year-old girl at a Bieber concert). To our pleasant surprise, she asked for our number and said she would call us to go backstage (then I acted like a 12-year-old who just *met* Bieber).

My wife and I, however, both thought there was no way she would actually follow through and call us. But she did! We went backstage and met every single member of the band. It was an incredible experience. All of a sudden, we were no longer faces in a crowd of thousands of people. We were somebodies. Guests. Individuals. Backstagers. VIPs!

That's what the inner circle is to you. That's the group you invite backstage behind the scenes. They should never feel like faces in the crowd. They should feel important.

Here's what I've learned: **backstage givers will make your fundraiser.** They are the smallest group, but they will give you the most money. If you don't handle the backstage people (the inner circle) correctly, you won't succeed in raising money.

STEP THREE: PLAN IT

In the next circle, put the names of people inside your network. This group represents your next level of relationships—Facebook friends, work friends, acquaintances, etc. Sticking with the concert analogy, this is the front-section fans. Front-section fans know most of the song lyrics. They'll buy a couple tickets when the band comes in town, but they wouldn't drive six hours to see them in another city like a backstage fan would. They'll buy a T-shirt and a poster, but they're not going to sponsor the band's next tour.

Another way of defining this group is by recognizing the people with whom you have a little relational equity, but they don't have as much financial margin. You won't know this about everyone. But you can make pretty good guesses. A schoolteacher may be generous, but he or she doesn't have the potential to drop a check as big as someone who owns an oil company. Again, it doesn't mean they're less important. But if they're not close friends or relatives, you would most likely place them in the second circle. The oil tycoon, on the other hand, goes straight into the inner circle.

Send a direct message to people in the second circle. An email, text, or possibly a phone call. They're important, so make sure you get information to them quickly.

In the last circle, put the names of people you're not relationally connected to. Or you're barely connected to. They are the crowd—the roaring audience who sits in the back. Because you're not close to them, you have no idea if they have financial margin or not. **Connect with this group by word-of-mouth or mass communication.** A lot of your contact with them will happen indirectly.

Here's the bottom line: good bands care about—and care for—their fans. They understand that people are the driving force behind their success. You must start seeing people as individuals. And as you already know, all individuals are different. Your one-page plan is simple, but people aren't. It's time to embrace the fact that if you're going to raise money, you need to connect with unique and complex human beings.

But what you'll discover along the way is that connecting with human beings makes life a lot more fun. And it makes your fundraising a lot more effective.

So, go get out your sheet of paper and start drawing some circles!

CHAPTER 13

INGREDIENT FIVE: A TARGETED MESSAGE

If you read the previous chapter, drew three circles, and filled them up with names, great job. I'm really proud of you. If you started scheduling coffee appointments and phone calls, I'm *really*, really proud of you!!! (Three exclamation points are a bit over the top, but I'm excited!)

Now, you have a big question to ask yourself. It's a question I've asked myself a lot: *What the heck am I going to say?* When I began speaking in front of people, I was terrible. Simply awful. I was nervous and self-conscious. I was sweaty and confusing (now that's a bad combo—sweaty *and* confusing). If you had heard me speak, you probably would've thought I was drunk. I wasn't . . . I just didn't know what to say. If I'd had the content, it would've given me confidence.

To connect with an audience or an individual, you have to understand what motivates them. Different people give to different things. There are trigger points that prompt certain people to action, but don't prompt others. Understanding those differences is vital to your plan.

1. **Some people are motivated by needs.** A clear need drives a lot of donors. I've heard people say, "People don't give to a need. They

give to a vision." While it's true that people give to a vision, it's probably truer that they give to a need. It's why people are moved when a natural disaster strikes and destroys a home. When they see a kid with no clothes or toys, they respond. It has nothing to do with a vision.

Needs are practical. Needs are tangible. Needs are attention-grabbing. No matter what method you use to raise money—a Kickstarter project, a golf tournament, *The One-Page Plan*, etc.—make sure you clearly identify your need. Instead of saying, "Give money to help kids with cancer," say, "We need $10,000 in 10 days to fund research for children who have cancer." People will respond better, because people respond to needs.

2. **Some people are motivated by vision.** When I say vision, I mean *preferred future*. Martin Luther King, Jr.'s "I Have a Dream" speech gave the world a clear picture of America's preferred future. His words inspired a nation. That's what vision has the power to do. This is particularly important for your backstage group of donors. Let the inner circle know where their dollars are going.

3. **Some people are motivated by relationships.** Picture this. You open the mail and receive two letters. One was mass-printed and mailed to you from an international hunger organization. The other was handwritten by your best friend's daughter, asking you to sponsor her trip to work with kids in an orphanage. Which are you more likely to sponsor? Hunger organizations are crucial, but your money will most likely go to the person you have a closer relationship with.

When it comes to relationships, you should never try to make a big withdrawal unless you've made a big deposit. As you prepare to launch your campaign to raise money, talk to people. Hang out with them. Get to know them. Don't blast stuff all over Twitter, make mass posts, and only talk about your dream. Make this process a two-way street. Make a relational investment of time and energy into the lives of your donors before you ask them to make a financial one into yours. And sure, you can ask strangers for money. But people who don't know you will not feel a personal burden to help you.

NEVER MAKE A BIG WITHDRAWL UNLESS YOU'VE MADE A BIG DEPOSIT

STEP THREE: PLAN IT

If you're currently thinking, *But I don't know what motivates my friends, family, and co-workers.* Don't panic. I say, do all three. Invest relationally, then concisely highlight the needs and the vision.

My hope is that you walk out of this section with confidence. *The One-Page Plan* creates simple steps so that you can be certain where you're going. When it comes to your messaging, you don't have to be a salesman, public speaker, or politician. You just have to be *you*, and really care about *them*.

CHAPTER 14

INGREDIENT SIX: AN EASY WAY TO GIVE

I love eating at Waffle House. I've been going there since I was a kid. There's nothing like a fiesta omelet with hash browns that have been scattered, smothered, and covered. The amount of grease in Waffle House meals is enough to kill an elephant. But in the South, we dig it. If you've never been to a Waffle House before, now is the time. You can thank me later.

I used to have a major problem with Waffle House—they were a cash-only establishment. I would show up ready to clog my arteries. Then I'd see the CASH ONLY sign. Then I'd get sad, turn around and leave. Sure, I could use an ATM and pay a terminal fee. But that was too much trouble. So, I'd go eat somewhere else.

In 2006, Waffle House made a big move. It purchased the technology to accept credit cards. Good for my appetite. Bad for my health.

We can all learn a lesson from Waffle House. They saw a problem and tackled it directly. They understood something that we as fundraisers get wrong all the time—if we make it complicated for people to give, they won't.

A couple of weeks ago, I spent an afternoon at a Barnes and Noble bookstore. I paid particular attention to people at the checkout lane. I wanted to see how many of them paid with cash. In two hours, I saw one person pull actual bills out of his wallet. Everyone else: swipe and go!

Over the last 10 years, research has shown a major decline in the use of cash. Just 50 years ago, cash accounted for eighty percent of domestic transactions. Today, that number is barely at fifty percent. Checks have fared even worse. That's probably not surprising news to you. But this probably is: cash and checks are still the main two ways people ask for donations.

We have to make it easy for people to give. Asking them to donate by cash or check only complicates the process. Complication leads to complexity. Complexity leads to confusion. Confusion leads to quitting. The last thing you want is for people to quit before they give.

An online giving system, however, isn't exactly the cure-all. I've seen some websites that require a doctorate-level degree to navigate. You have to click 10 times before you get to the actual donation page. Then you have to create an online account. Sometimes you also have to then activate that account in order to give. It makes me tired just thinking about it!

In 2012, Mitt Romney ran against President Obama in one of the most publicized elections in the history of the world. My team and I did some research that year. We got on both candidates' websites to see which one made it easiest to donate money. This isn't a political plug, but President Obama's site was significantly easier to navigate. It took us 74 seconds to give on his page. Mitt Romney's page took us 20 seconds longer. It came as no surprise to us that the person with the easier website raised more money for his campaign.

We looked at church websites, too. In fact, we donated money to 100 churches. The average online giving time was three minutes. That's too long. Non-profit websites were even worse. Listen, we *have* to make it easier for donors to give.

You may be reading this book because you want a simple plan for raising money for your dream. Maybe you're tired of over-complicated plans. If that's the case, then you understand the importance of sim-

STEP THREE: PLAN IT

plicity. Now put yourself in the shoes of your donors: they want the same thing. Maybe the success of your campaign depends on how easy you make it for them to give. Don't worry, we will help you every step of the way.

Once you get that figured out, the runway for your campaign will be ready. Now it's time to fly!

SECTION IV

THE ONE-PAGE PLAN
STEP FOUR: DO IT

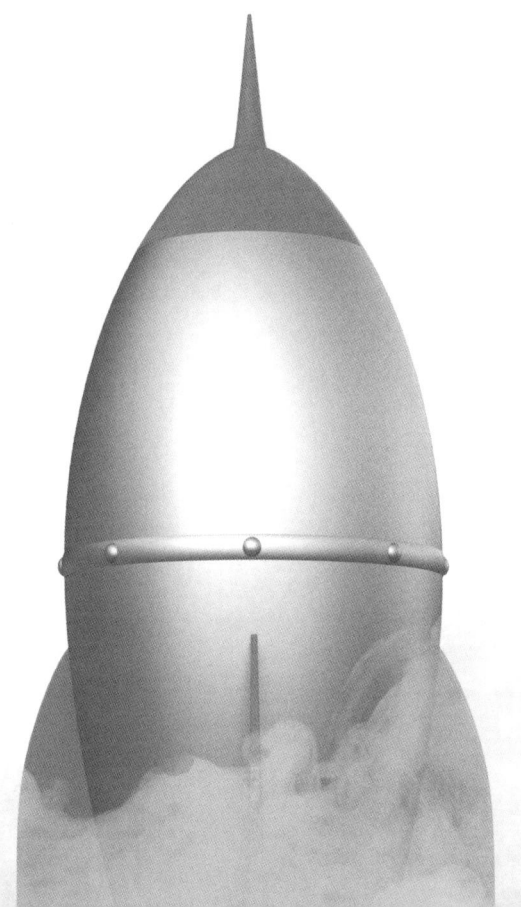

CHAPTER 15

1 ASK TRUMPS 1,000 HINTS

I love the phrase: *Get fired up!* I get a strange satisfaction out of saying it. And I always put an exclamation point when I type it. It's basically a redneck way of saying get excited, get motivated, or celebrate. With that being said, I want you to get fired up! If you've tracked with me through this book so far, you've done something that most fundraisers never do—built your very own workable plan. Creating a custom fundraising strategy is a huge deal.

In my opinion, the *planning* is the hard part. You've done that. Now, we get to the fun part—*doing*. Just typing that sentence turns up my obnoxious-meter a level:

GET FIRED UP!

Let's recap where we've been. You have . . .
- Owned it
- Clarified it
- Planned it

Now, it's time to do it!

Just do it. Nike coined it perfectly, didn't they? Speaking of Nike, I loved the '94 Air Jordan shoes back in the day. If you don't know what I'm talking about, you were probably in your high school marching band. If you were in your high school marching band, I bet you played your instrument a lot better than I played basketball in those Jordans.

Back to the point. Planning is great. But here's the thing about planning: Planning itself has never raised a single dollar. Yesterday, I sat down with the CEO of a non-profit that raises millions of dollars each year through donations. He and I spent some time talking about his development team.

In the non-profit sector, the development team is supposed to raise money. Trouble is, they usually don't. Now, I'm not against development people. They're awesome. But it's been my experience that they usually have a plan, but they rarely execute it well. As I talked with this particular CEO, he spoke highly of the people on his development team, but he voiced one concern: they didn't produce. Great people, low production.

I've heard that story a lot. Development people place high value on relational development, but they have little concern for financial development.

I don't know about you, but I care a lot more about deposits than I do about developments.

Before you think I'm an evil fundraising guy, here's what I mean. If you want to fund your dream, you must have money. You can't use "development" to buy a cup of coffee at Starbucks. No, you need cash or as I've already observed, at least a debit card. As fundraisers, we have bought into the idea that development is the end game. And while developing givers is important, it's not crucial. I see this in businesses, non-profits, and kickstarters all the time. People focus on developing relationships and giving key information to potential donors. But they don't take one vital step: asking for money.

> PLANNING ITSELF HAS NEVER RAISED A SINGLE DOLLAR

One of the biggest fundraising mistakes you can make is to raise a lot of awareness but very little money. One day, I met with a guy who was starting a church. Here's how he set up the meeting: "I'd love to just

STEP FOUR: DO IT

catch up with you." If you're raising money, you might as well be clear. Everybody knows you want money. "I'd love to catch up" is code for "I want your cash."

I liked the guy, so I went. The meeting was supposed to last one hour. I drank black coffee that cost $2.08 while he talked for 70 minutes straight. He told me about all the cool stuff he was doing. He described the way he was going to plant his church. He explained some of the charity work he was doing for his community. I gained a lot of awareness.

At about the 73-minute mark, I said, "Hey, I need to go. I have another meeting I need to drive to." He got visibly awkward. He started saying things like, "Well, if you want to be a part of the stuff I was telling you about, let me know." I could tell he was uncomfortable. But because I've been in his shoes before, I knew that he wanted money. So I asked him, "Are you asking me for money?" He fumbled around for another two minutes, so I asked him again, "Are you asking me to give you money or not?"

> **WHEN IT COMES TO RAISING MONEY, ONE ASK IS BETTER THAN A THOUSAND HINTS**

When he finally muttered, "Yes," I looked at him and said, "Well, why didn't you ask me an hour ago? We could have saved all this time. How much do you want me to give?" No answer. I suggested an amount. He said, "That's awesome. Thank you so much." I would've given him more because he's such a good guy, but he had no idea how to ask for money.

For an hour, I listened to a guy who was really good at *hinting*, when he should've been great at *asking*. Because when it comes to raising money, one ask is better than a thousand hints.

After you've created your plan, you must go out and ask. How do you do that? Simple. You say:

"Will you give us _____ dollars by _____?"

People question me on this all the time. They want to know if I really ask people to give a specific amount. Yes, I do. I don't say to people, "Just give what you can." Because **people give as little as they can when you ask them to give what they can.** It's the way people are wired. They think about what's comfortable. And "comfortable" is always the smallest amount of money possible. Your job as a fundraiser is to challenge people with a specific amount, and then let them decide or adjust from there.

- "Will you give $1,000 by next Wednesday?" is infinitely more effective than, "Would you be interested in being a part at some level?"
- "I'd love for you to give $500 by this time next week" is better than "Go think about it and just give what you can."

This step in *The One-Page Plan* is titled Do It, which means it's time to take action. This entire book may be a waste of time if you're not willing to take a deep breath, look someone in the eye, and ask for money. If you're hoping to raise money without directly asking for it, you will never fund your dream.

I have a challenge for you, just to practice: ask somebody for money right now. Spouses not included (although for some of you, asking your spouse would be much more frightening than asking a random stranger!). And don't ask your mother-in-law . . . unless you have a really cool mother-in-law. Think of someone you wish would give money to your vision, and then call him or her.

Yeah, I know you don't *want* to, but you really need to.

Ask them for $100. Right now. No, literally, right this second. Quit arguing with me in your mind. And quit coming up with crazy excuses. "I hate talking on the phone" is *not* a good reason to avoid this exercise. It doesn't matter if they say yes or no. What matters is that you practice making the ask.

No hinting allowed. Get fired up and start *asking!*

CHAPTER 16

ASKING PRIVATELY > ASKING PUBLICLY

My social media accounts are full of people asking for money. Here are some of the requests for money I've gotten in the last few weeks:

- Making a Christmas album
- Writing a social networking book
- Starting a T-shirt company

I could go on and on. The public ask for money is as common as a Taylor Swift breakup song. I call it the *Mass Ask*. It's the most common type of request for money these days. People say things like, "If every one of our followers would only give $3, we'd raise all the money."

Let me save you time. This doesn't work.

When you publically broadcast invitations, you may feel like you're making an ask. But you aren't. The *Mass Ask* is easy, but it's not effective. Sure, you may hear of an isolated campaign that worked through mass posts and texts. But 99.9% of them don't. Here's why.

- *People get hidden in the numbers.* When I see your Facebook post, I know that a lot of other people do, too. So I don't feel the pressure to give, because I assume that other people are responding. But they're not. Because they, like me, aren't really being asked.

- *People give in low amounts.* Even if you get donations through mass invites, you will most likely attract low-level donors who give the bare minimum. It seems heroic for you to say, "If everyone only gave $3. . . . " But if I was planning on giving you $15, it's easy for me to cut that back to $3. After all, that's what you asked me to give.

- *The 20/80 rule.* In most fundraising I've seen, twenty percent of the people give eighty percent of the money. My opinion is that if you spend eighty percent of your time and energy creating a mass marketing campaign, you will reach twenty percent of your potential. Sure, some people will give. But you'll miss a greater opportunity.

EASY ROUTE = ASKING PUBLICALLY
EFFECTIVE ROUTE = ASKING PRIVATELY

When most people hear the word *private*, they think of off-limits. I live in a small town in Georgia. There are farms, chickens, goats, and horses everywhere. A lot of these properties have signs that say, PRIVATE PROPERTY DO NOT ENTER. You're free to disobey this warning, but I promise you will get shot. Like, with a real shotgun. My theory is that private property signs are really code for *Don't expect to trespass and live to tell about it.*

Also, my family grew up with a saying: Don't talk about money or religion. I questioned that saying one time. The response I got: "Because those things are private."

My point is people are intimidated by the word private. When I talk about asking for money privately, it scares most people. People equate it to parents explaining to their 12-year-old where babies come from.

But here's why private is so powerful. If you get invited to a private party, you feel special. You feel important. You have access to a party that other people don't have access to. You're a trusted friend—that's why you were invited. When you think about it that way, private isn't a

STEP FOUR: DO IT

bad word. It's a great one, especially when it comes to raising money. You will get eighty percent of the money from twenty percent of the donors... that you ask in private.

My family supports two Compassion International children. One kid is from Nicaragua and the other is from Africa. We give monthly to support them. I would love to say that the reason I started giving to Compassion was to help kids in need, but it's not. Sure, I love the idea of helping kids, but there are a hundred other organizations doing the same thing. My motivation came from somewhere else.

A few years back I was invited by a friend to go on a Compassion trip. My friend's organization paid for everything. Along with 20 other people, I observed a couple of places where Compassion operates overseas. As you can imagine, that experience made it easy for me to give to Compassion. But in the end, I went on that trip because I trust my friend, not because of my heart for kids in need. And I give to Compassion because my friend trusts them.

People give to people. Sure, the dream, cause, or business matters. But not as much as you think. Your best donations will come from people you already know who already trust you. Rarely will you have a random person give you a boatload of money.

So yes, develop great relationships. Every social media relationship matters. Every family member matters. Every single person you have ever known matters. But you still have to make the ask. And you still need to do it personally.

So, what is a private ask? Here are a few I've done that work really well.

1. **Private meetings.** This is simple but scary. Invite your closest friends to dinner, coffee, or to your home. Tell them *in advance* what you want to talk about. Say something like, "I'd love to meet with you about _____ *(your campaign)* and speak with you about your involvement at some level." Assure them that there's no pressure, but you'd like the opportunity to speak with them about it.

   When you meet with potential donors in person, please act normal. I beg you. Sure, you might be a little nervous. But nervous doesn't mean you should turn into a seventh-grader at the Spring Dance. Since your potential donor already knows what the meeting is about, just be upfront and honest.

A few common mistakes (trust me, I've learned from making them):

- **Over-talking.** Don't sit around and shoot the breeze for 45 minutes, then squeeze your ask into the last 15. That makes people uncomfortable. Chat 5-10 minutes about life, sports, movies, kids, politics, or whatever you want to chat about. Then ask if you can jump in.

- **Over-informing.** Like I already stated, most of the time, people don't meet you because they're huge believers in what you're doing. I know this is hard to believe because you're so passionate about your dream. But most people are there simply because you invited them. So, take about 10 minutes to cast clear vision about WHY you're doing what you're doing, and then show them WHAT their money will be going toward. That's it.

One time, I was raising money for an area destroyed by a tornado. I told donors: "I'm doing this because the thought of a kid going without basic needs for the next 48 hours bothers me deeply. I'm asking you to give money that will go to immediate relief for these children." Most human beings would give money to that. They didn't need to know everything. They needed to know my heart, and my plan for their money.

Sure, you can make it more conversational than that. But remember, **people don't care about the details as much as they care about you.** If they are willing to meet you one-on-one, they already trust you to some level.

2. **Private messages.** I've raised more money using text messages than anything else. Texting people that I already have a good relationship with and asking them for support—it works like magic.

Here's why I have the confidence to ask people privately: the ask isn't for me. I'm not asking for money just to make my life better. I'm asking to help other people. With that in the forefront of my mind, anytime I raise money, I use texts, direct messages on Twitter and Facebook, and direct emails.

STEP FOUR: DO IT

To review, here are a few reasons why you should ask privately for money:

- People feel responsible when you ask them personally.
- People will have to make a decision.
- People respond to feeling needed.

Do you spend your time attempting public or private asks? I suggest you spend eighty percent of your time taking the one-on-one approach. At the end of this section, we'll help you establish a great plan to do this. This step in *The One-Page Plan* will be a game-changer for the rest of your fundraising life!

CHAPTER 17

WHY A SPECIFIC ASK BEATS A GENERAL ASK

When I got married, I lived like I was still single. I threw clothes on the floor. I left piles of dishes in the sink. I had a couple of dude roomies during my pre-marriage years that no one would confuse with clean. Our strategy was to create exclusive piles of clothes and dishes. When both piles were maxed out, we'd put a Pearl Jam album in the CD player and have a "cleaning day." The idea of cleaning every day . . . *every day* . . . what? . . . are you kidding me? In no universe would I be the kind of guy who tidied up on a daily basis.

Then I got married.

My wife and I would go on dates and talk about our marriage. We'd discuss things that we needed to work on and improve. Kacie would consistently say things like, "I'd like for you to help out more around the house."

It sounds crazy (and you're more than welcome to make fun of me), but I didn't know what she meant. To me, it was *normal* to have four weeks worth of clothes piled up on the floor. The house was still clean in my eyes. My clean and her clean were as different as salsa dancing and breakdancing (now that I think about it, I'd love to try to combine those two at the next wedding reception I attend!).

My wife's awesome. She's a very orderly person. She's the type of person who can't go to bed with dishes in the sink. Not me. I can sleep fine. I could probably sleep with dirty dishes *in* my bed. Needless to say, we fought about this a lot in the early years of our marriage.

One time, in the midst of an argument, I asked, "What isn't clean about this house?" That was a stupid question. In my mind, I was comparing our house to baseball locker rooms and apartments I had lived in with complete slobs. Our house was the cleanest place I had occupied in years. I really wanted to be a good husband, but "help out more around the house" wasn't registering with me.

One day we were hanging out with another couple, and we told them about our little cleaning conflict. Okay, *big* cleaning conflict. They had dealt with the same issue, so they coached us on how to make things better. It started with my wife (see, I knew it wasn't my fault!). They told Kacie that she had to be outrageously literal with me and say things like, "I need all of the dishes out of the sink by midnight tonight." Seems ridiculous, right? I mean, does she really have to hold my hand and give me instructions like I was a highly distracted seven-year-old? Yes. She does. I love it. And now she does, too.

We're almost a decade into marriage. By now, my role is clearly defined. If my wife wants me to do something, she knows that I will if she asks me like this: "Will you please fold all of the laundry in the dryer before I get home?"

Being specific about roles around the house has created way less tension in our marriage. In the same way, being specific when you raise money will create way less stress in your campaign.

My friend, Jeff Henderson, did this really well in a recent letter he sent me. He was raising money for a friend's adoption, and he decided to send letters to a few, specific people. One thing this letter had was handwriting on the envelope. Not labels—but actual pen on paper writing. I will always open a handwritten envelope. On the other hand, I will always put a labeled envelope in the *To Read Later Pile.*

So whenever possible, handwrite your envelopes. Here's the second cool thing this letter did: it stated how many people Jeff sent it to.

STEP FOUR: DO IT

When I read this and saw that I was part of a small, select group, I felt included. This helped me feel personally connected to what the letter was asking.

The last thing Jeff's letter did was ask every donor to give at least $500 to his friend's cause. He said, "You can give as much as you want. But please at least give $500." Jeff set a baseline.

For most people who raise money, the baseline is $0. Not Jeff. The last I checked, his letters alone had raised $10,000.

There's nothing as frustrating as someone who plans well, but then chickens out because they're afraid to ask people for a specific dollar amount. Keep in mind, you create the floor for your fundraiser. Jeff's floor was $500. One thing I've learned is that people will give close to what you ask them to give. Especially your high-capacity givers.

This doesn't mean you can get on social media and ask everyone for $10,000 (well, you *can*, I just don't know how effective it would be). No, your amounts will be different based on the category of your donor. Create a clear baseline that is appropriate for each group.

I've had the most success with specific asks when I've given people three options. For example, I've asked people to give either $250, $500, or $1,000. Sometimes it's helpful to put the amount you really want people to choose in the middle. People don't want to appear cheap. On the other hand, the majority isn't likely to pick the highest tier. Most people will default to the middle level.

Often, I'll name my tiers. For example, the $250 tier may be called the Affiliate Level. $500 is the Partnership Level. And the $1,000-givers are in the Legacy Level. Naming your tiers gives people a personal connection to the amount they are donating.

In addition to naming your tiers, you should also break down how many people you need to participate in each one. For example, if you're raising $10,000, you'll need five Legacy givers, five Partners, and 10 Affiliates. You can inform people of this through social media and in person.

Finally, it's great if you can provide potential donors with a graphic that visually represents your need. For example:

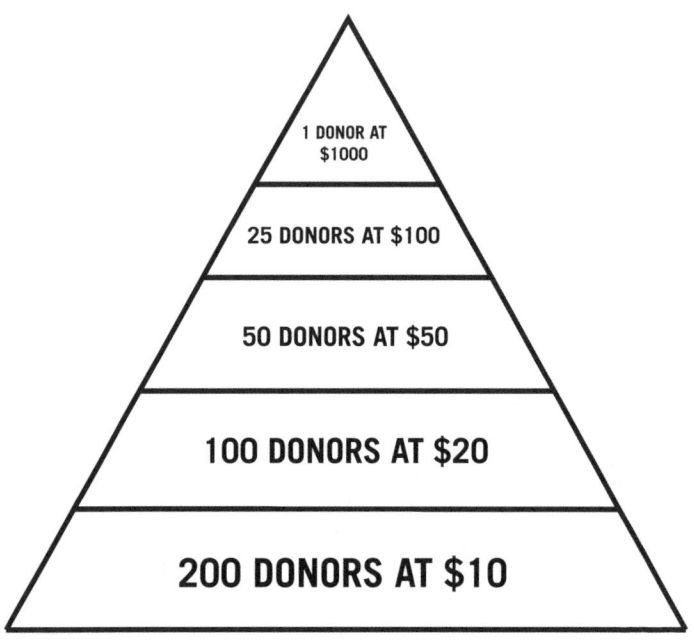

Using this chart, donors can get a picture of how their $100 can pave the way for you to reach your fundraising goal.

I saw a pastor do this once. He showed the entire church his picture of the tiers. He said, in a humble yet confident way: "Pick the tier that feels most comfortable to you. Then go one tier up. Stretch yourself." He asked them to give more than they typically would. And you know what? They did exactly that.

Nothing will kill your fundraiser faster than your unwillingness to ask specifically. It's a muscle that you have to build. Trust me, it does get easier with experience. Over time, you'll also get more comfortable creating tiers and graphics to aid your campaign. But the only way to get better at it is to DO IT! We will help you every step of the way.

CHAPTER 18

ASK ONE TO MAKE TWO

When it comes to raising money, this chapter is about the best trick in my bag. If you don't like calling it a trick, you can call it a tactic, concept, tip, or technique. In fact, just call it whatever you want. The point is, it works. I accidentally stumbled upon this simple idea years ago. Since then, it's been revolutionary.

In a previous chapter, I told you to identify some prospective donors who could potentially give you a larger-than-average sum of money. I also told you to ask them to give a *specific* amount. All of that is great. Now, I want you to take it one step further.

From that group, I want you to pick two or three people and ask them to be matching donors. In other words, ask them to match what you raise dollar-for-dollar within a certain time period. Whether or not you put a cap on the amount is up to you (and dependent on the donor). You might ask him or her, "Between 8:00 p.m. and midnight tonight, will you match every dollar I raise up to $1,000?"

When these types of donors commit to your campaign, something magical happens: I call it the *Matching Triangle.* The Matching Triangle puts three parties—you, your matching donor, and your larger donor pool—at peak states.

You. For you, the matching donor idea automatically puts traction behind your campaign. When you unveil it to the team you're working with, it puts new momentum, excitement, and energy into your fundraising.

Matching Donor. For your matching donor, it makes them feel like a hero. They are set apart—different—from other givers. In an instant, they find themselves in a giving tier that is exclusively theirs. They believe that they are integral to your campaign . . . because they are! For every dollar they give, they're really giving two. Plus, you don't have to ask for a check right then and there. It's easier to get people to commit to *future* giving than *present* giving.

The Donor Pool. Finally, donor matching is good for your donor pool. You take it straight to your social media outlets and raise the flag. For people who have been thinking about giving but haven't, a matching donor, and the thought of doubling their contribution, will push them to act.

When it comes to raising money, these three parts are like the three main parts of a human brain. Did you ever study them in school? We did, even in rural Alabama. Their scientific names may have changed since then, but I remember them as the *cerebrum, cerebellum,* and the *medulla oblongata* (cue Bobby Boucher from the movie *Waterboy!*). When those three pieces come together, there is no more powerful device in humanity than the human brain.

I recently got a text message from the founders of So Worth Loving, a non-profit organization that promotes self-worth and self-acceptance. Through social media, I was aware that they were trying to raise money for a So Worth Loving Tour. But they were stuck.

The goal was $27,000. But they had hit their cap and couldn't seem to raise another cent. I was in the middle of writing this section, so I decided once again to put my trick to the test. I told them I'd match every dollar up to $500 if they raised it by midnight that night. You wouldn't believe the mayhem that followed. They got on Instagram, Twitter, Facebook, Vine, and every other social media outlet you can imagine. They let everyone know they had a matching donor (and the ability to raise some decent money that very night).

STEP FOUR: DO IT

In four hours they raised $600, which translated to $1,200. $600 was more than they had raised in the previous four days combined. Why? Because it put them and their donors back into urgent launch mode. That's what matching donors do—they create mini-explosions that continuously infuse your campaign with exhilaration.

The challenge I have for you right now is simple. Find a matching donor. Clearly explain the match. Then boldly make the ask. And make sure to keep this little trick in your bag!

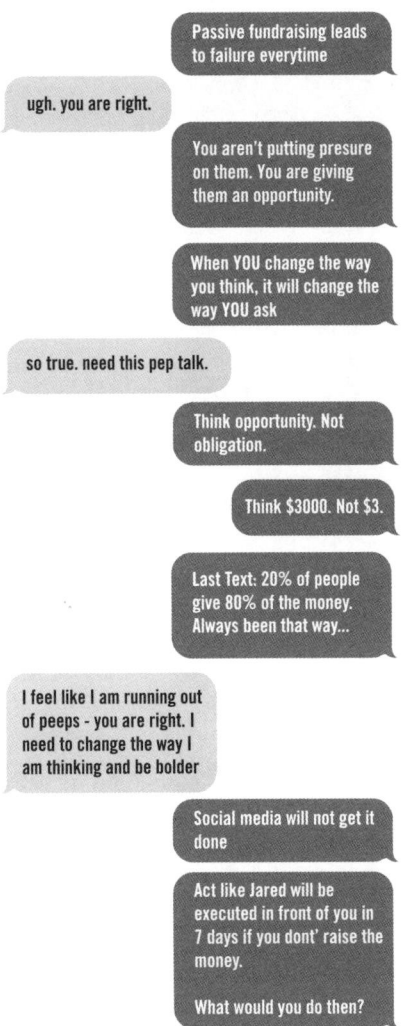

Text Messages between So Worth Loving founder Eryn Eddy and myself.

CHAPTER 19

ASK DONORS TO GIVE TO DEADLINES

If you're anything like most people — chronic procrastinators — this concept will challenge you. I'm always waiting until the last minute to do things. Whether it's obligations with friends or family, I never seem to find the time to accomplish anything early.

Instead, I am driven by deadlines.

This mindset, however, is lethal when it comes to fundraising. It doesn't work. You can't wait until the last minutes to raise the money you need. If you do that, people are going to feel pressured. They haven't heard from you in weeks or months, then all the sudden you're beating down their doors via Twitter, text, phone, or their literal front door. You're begging them to give, and your sense of urgency makes you seem pushy, desperate, or unorganized.

Or, it makes you seem creepy. No one wants to be creepy.

Understanding how to appropriately apply deadlines in your fundraiser will take your campaign from average to a homerun. The solution to procrastinating in fundraising is easy: Act like it's the last day every day. So many people do an incredible job of directly asking on the last day. They create a sense of urgency because their time is up. But in order for your fundraiser to be successful from top to bottom, you must treat *every day* of your campaign as if it were the last. This takes energy, focus, consistency, and perpetual motivation. But the rewards far exceed the work.

> **THE SOLUTION TO PROCRASTINATING IN FUNDRAISING IS EASY: ACT LIKE IT'S THE LAST DAY EVERY DAY**

We've already said that you must establish a fundraising deadline. That's true. Date and dollar amounts are paramount. But that date can't be your only deadline—it's just your *ultimate* deadline. Just because that ending point is on your calendar doesn't mean you should wait until that day to measure the success of your campaign. No, what you need are mini-deadlines along that way that keep your funds rolling in at a sustainable pace.

Remember, deadlines drive donors. Think about that word: *DEADline.* The word itself suggests that some type of death will occur if the line is crossed. So according to this chapter so far, you will either be dead or a creep if you don't set deadlines. So, I guess you better get moving!

Okay, okay. Maybe no one will die if you miss your deadline, but there will likely be pain and frustration.

But you can also use that to your advantage. This may sound insensitive, but it's true: People will give you money just to get you off their back. In order to avoid the pain of a deadline you've given them, they will send a check so they can be done with it and mark it off their list. I'm not saying that you should be manipulative with your fundraising. I'm just saying that deadlines push donors to pull the trigger.

Earlier in this book, we talked about three different levels of givers: the backstage crowd, the front row crowd, and the rest of the audience. Each of these groups requires a different deadline. One huge mistake fundraisers make is creating the same deadline for everyone—the last day of the campaign. If you only adhere to one ultimate end date, it will spell trouble. If the bank account remains stagnant at the finish line, you can be confident that your blood pressure will go up. You need the momentum of little deadlines along the way so it doesn't all come down to the last drive of the fourth quarter.

For example, you want the higher-level donors to give first. This is your

STEP FOUR: DO IT

backstage group. These are the folks who could potentially be your matching donors. You do this for a couple of reasons. One, you don't want to get close to your ultimate deadline with a mere *hope* that these people will actually give. You want to know yes or no long before that. Why? Because you don't want to depend on money that may never show up. Knowing where you stand with your bigger givers helps you gauge the rest of your campaign.

When you send an email or text—or when you meet with donors in person—your verbiage should be clear and precise: "I'm asking you to give $2,000 by this Friday." Even if you don't really need that money for a month, you want to set your deadline for them before they become the deadline for you.

> ABOVE ALL, TREAT EACH DAY AS IF IT WERE THE LAST DAY OF YOUR CAMPAIGN

If the person you're asking for money says they need to confer with someone else or "check on some things" before they commit, be sure to ask specifically when you can follow up. Say something like: "Hey, that's no problem at all. Thanks for checking. When can I follow up with you about this?" Their answer to that question gives you permission to call without feeling like a jerk. "Hey, it's Casey. I told you I would call you today about the project we discussed. I just wanted to see if you made a decision."

Remember, it's your job to provide clarity for every donor. People should never be confused about how much you want them to give and by when.

To recap, there are two types of deadlines you must manage:

1. **Mini Deadlines.** One of the worst things you can do as a fundraiser is say, "I need $50,000 in 90 days," and then do a mass ask every day until the allotted time is up. To me, it's much more effective to break that up into a goal of $555 a day. Sales teams do this all the time. They set annual, quarterly, monthly, weekly, and yes, daily goals. If they waited until December to measure their sales, it would be way too late to strategize ways to close the gap between their goals and their current situation. Mini deadlines keep you motivated and your donors on track.

2. **Ultimate Deadline.** All of the mini deadlines should lead up to this deadline. This is the Olympic finals. You'll either win a gold medal and grace the cover of a Wheaties® box, or you'll go back to being a drill operator in Prudhoe Bay, Alaska, and nobody will even know you competed.

Be diligent. Be clear. Above all, treat each day as if it were the last day of your campaign.

CHAPTER 20

CREATE A LIST OF PEOPLE TO ASK

You have everything you need to ask people for money. My question for you is:

WILL YOU ACTUALLY DO IT?

Pick up your phone right now. Open your contacts. Start a list (NO, REALLY, START A LIST) of people you can ask for money. As you're jotting down their names, make a note as to which section you think they're in—backstage, front row, or crowd.

After that, open up your social media accounts. Add to your list.

Use any database you have access to. Add to your list.

Now put away your freaking book, iPad, or e-reader and call some people. Get a lunch on the calendar. Schedule a meeting. Fill up your calendar and make this thing happen!

If you need help, check out our website **FundraisingRocket.com/tools**. Here, you'll find all the resources, training videos, and additional materials you could ever want.

You've taken some huge steps in *The One-Page Plan*. I'm proud of you. You've owned it. You've clarified it. You've planned it. Now, my friend, get out there and DO IT!

SECTION V

THE ONE-PAGE PLAN
STEP FIVE: CELEBRATE IT

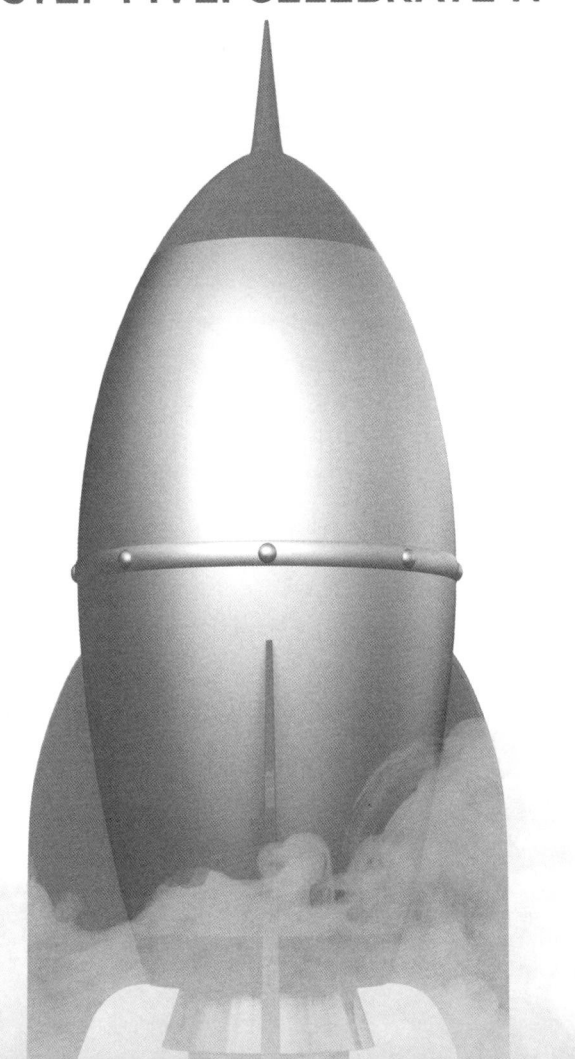

CHAPTER 21

REMEMBER: THEY FUNDED YOUR DREAM

Most people want to skip this section because they see it as total fluff. If that's you, then you need to read this section . . . 74 times. Memorize the whole thing. Pound this philosophy into your head: the only way to win in fundraising is to celebrate people.

If you've owned it, clarified it, planned it, and then made it happen, great job! You are a *One-Page Plan* rock star! But . . . if you do all of that and somehow neglect this step, your plan is still lacking. Unsuccessful. Futile.

An unwritten or unsent thank-you note feels like a slap in the face. I can't overemphasize how important this is: **feeling grateful is different from actually saying "thank you."** You need to say it! And I'm not just referring to people who've given you money. I'm referring to *anyone* who has emotionally supported you, retweeted you, or passed your information along. Thank your team. Thank your volunteers. Shoot, thank your mama while you're at it. Call her up and thank her for giving birth to you. My mama gave birth to me in a rural Alabama hospital.

> THE ONLY WAY TO WIN IN FUNDRAISING IS TO CELEBRATE PEOPLE

And I bet that was no walk in the park back in the 70s!

Here's why this step is so impactful—because grateful people are rare. Being a thankful human being is not commonplace. Our society moves at such a quick pace that it's very challenging for us to:
- pause our progress,
- use our manners,
- and adequately give thanks.

But we have to wake up. Think about it—many of your supporters took hard-earned dollars out of *their* bank accounts and gave them to you to fund your dream or cause. That's a big, big, big, big deal!

Perhaps the problem is that saying "thank you" seems irrelevant. Most of us learned to say it when we were two years old. Our parents taught us to be "polite." But as adults, we often brush off its significance. Or we offer a shallow, mindless "thanks." Or, most commonly, we forget altogether.

Not only is expressing gratitude the right thing to do, it's the savvy thing to do. If you want to have . . .
- more fundraising projects in the future,
- credibility with the people who supported your campaign,
- and happy donors

Then you must add more value to people's lives than just taking their money.

One mistake made by a lot of fundraisers is to make their campaign all about *people* before the money is raised, and all about *dollar amounts* afterward. There's obviously nothing wrong with celebrating amounts raised, causes funded, and goals accomplished, but we need to be very careful not to make it only about money and agendas. After your campaign is over, share stories of people who gave. Mention actual names if appropriate. Talk about the kid who emptied his piggybank, the family who gave despite financial hardship, and the team member who volunteered countless hours. If you're all about people on the front end, you have to be all about them on the back end.

How much energy do you put into asking for money? You should put that much energy into celebrating people. One way I've done this is by consistently honoring a *Person of the Day* on Instagram. Every other day, I'll choose someone to praise publically. I'll ask other people to

STEP FIVE: CELEBRATE IT

praise them, too. At first I was worried that people would find it cheesy. But then I remembered: I'm a cheesy person (I'm always so relieved when I remember that). I love cheese—the food and the sappy emotional sentiment. So, then I quit worrying about it.

I've discovered that it's been a big deal to people, and here's why: because people get beaten down. They're tired, stressed, overworked, and underpaid. And they need to be encouraged. They need to be bragged on. They need to be valued.

I firmly believe that saying "thank you" is good for *them*, but I think it's better for you. Not just in fundraising, but in all areas of your life. It keeps you humble. It keeps you from being selfish and arrogant. It keeps you from being a person whose calls are screened by others. Saying "thank you" softens your heart.

In case you missed the point, *they* funded *your* dream. And because they emptied their pocketbook for you, you should fill their lives with gratitude and celebration. When you think you've celebrated too much, you've just gotten started. You can't celebrate your team, donors, or supporters enough.

This is a step in *The One-Page Plan* that you can't afford to gloss over. Want to know how to do it effectively? Keep reading.

CHAPTER 22

10 CREATIVE WAYS TO SAY "THANK YOU"

Maybe you've heard the saying, "The road to hell is paved with good intentions." I'm sitting here wondering if my editor will let me start a chapter with that quote. But I use it because I don't want you to read this book, get inspired and think: *These are good ideas. I should try them sometime.* No, I want you to read this book and act! Because when it comes to raising money, good intentions are the pathway to failure.

No one feels thanked because you had *intentions* to say "thank you." They feel thanked because you actually thanked them. Many people skip this step because it feels so overwhelming. But it doesn't have to feel that way. You don't have to throw a huge banquet or party. You just have to take a step.

That's what this chapter is about—giving you some ideas on how to show gratitude. This isn't an exhaustive list by any means. I'm not trying to "wow" anyone with this list. I'm trying to show you how simple and practical this step can be.

Before we start the list, I want to reiterate: **the smallest action of**

gratitude is better than the greatest intention.

> ACTION > INTENTION

With that being said, let's get fired up and put this in action!

1. **The Handwritten Thanks.** This is one of the most powerful things you can do. Write a note to everyone who supported you. Don't start whining like you're in freshman English class. It doesn't have to be a novel; a couple of sentences will do. And don't use bad handwriting as an excuse, either. Remember, *these are people who funded your dream!* Postage, paper, and a little time are a small price to pay. One last thought—don't use labels. Handwrite their name and address on the front of the envelope.

2. **The Candy Thanks.** Send people their favorite candy. Simple enough. Text their spouse or best friend—or look on social media—to find out what they love. Then mail them the biggest bag you can possibly find. To take this over the top, get on Pinterest (a great place to take *anything* over the top) and find cheesy sayings that connect the candy to your thanks. Or, like we've already mentioned, include a handwritten note.

3. **The Steak Thanks.** This one is easy. Send some Omaha Steaks in the mail. It's perfect for guys who love to cook on the grill. It's also great for families. The wow factor comes from the way Omaha Steaks are delivered. They show up in dry ice on the front porch, and it looks like a bigger deal than it really is. The added benefit comes when recipients post about your gift on Facebook, Instagram, or Twitter.

4. **The Date Thanks.** Send a complete date night package to a couple. This can include a gift card to a restaurant, a movie gift card, and cash for a babysitter. Provide the stuff that takes the guesswork out of an evening together. Obviously, you can't do this for everyone. But when you can, it makes couples feel valued and appreciated.

5. **The Personal Thanks.** In the last section, we talked about the importance of a direct, personal ask. In the same way, a face-to-face, eye-to-eye "thank you" is meaningful and effective.

6. **The Text Bomb Thanks.** Choose someone who gave to your campaign—let's say, Bob. Coordinate with Bob's friends to send him a

STEP FIVE: CELEBRATE IT

ton of texts within a short period of time. Make sure you tell Bob's friends that the purpose of these texts are to tell Bob how generous and awesome he is. The more friends who participate, the bigger the impact.

7. **The Public Thanks.** Get on Facebook, Instagram or Twitter and post someone's picture. You could say something like, "This guy/girl made a huge difference in getting clean water to a village in Kenya." Or, "This family played a huge role in helping me launch my business and pursue my dream." Whether people gave a little or a lot, it's great to publicly affirm them.

8. **The Story Thanks.** Find a person who benefited from the money that was contributed and tell their story. For instance, if you raised money so needy kids could receive medical attention, find a story of a child whose condition improved through treatment. Then, write the story as if it's coming from that kid. In some cases, the person who was helped can write the story themselves. That's great. Then, share it with everyone who supported the campaign. Remind them that *they* made it happen. Celebrate the win, not the money.

9. **The Phone Thanks.** Pick up the phone and dial someone's number. I encourage you to do it immediately after they give. Even if they don't answer, leave a voicemail with a heartfelt "thank you."

10. **The Party Thanks.** This is a common celebration for larger campaigns. But if you decide to throw a party, make it fun. Make it relational. Okay, I'll just say it—*don't make it stuffy and boring!* It's fine to get up and talk. But keep it short and to the point. Say "thank you" and share a story or a win. Don't draw it out and show a million photos. Sometimes the best way to say "thank you" is by allowing people to have a good time.

These options range from free to expensive. And the time commitments range from a minute to a month. Like I said earlier, you may come up with a better idea. If you do, that's awesome. Please go for it. What I *don't* want you to do, however, is make excuses. Or have good intentions with no follow-through. *The One-Page Plan* is simply incomplete without this step. So take action, because action > intention.

MY THANK YOU LIST

List of People to ThankHow I Will Thank Them

To take this step to the next level, go to **FundraisingRocket.com/tools**. Seriously, go . . . now . . . please!

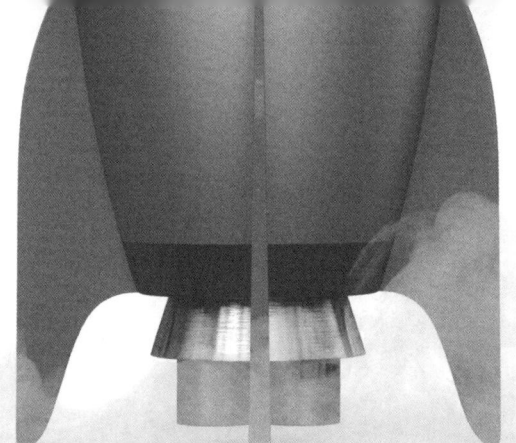

CONCLUSION
YOU CAN CHANGE THE WORLD

THINK BIG. ACT SMALL.

A lot of people talk about changing the world.

That's awesome, but what does it mean? No, literally, what does it mean? How is it realistically going to happen? People who say they want to change the world are typically great people with big hearts. But that phrase is too vague and general to get them anywhere. I've seen it time and time again.

I love to think big. If we sat down and you told me that your fundraiser was going to change the entire world, I'd fully support you. If my daughter said, "Daddy, I want to do something to help the whole universe," I'd throw every resource I could in her direction.

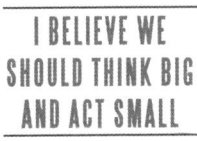
I BELIEVE WE SHOULD THINK BIG AND ACT SMALL

But most likely, you're not going to change THE world. You're going to change A world. And you must have the mindset that changing A world is just as important.

We need to get back to the basics of why we raise money in the first place. What are we hoping to accomplish? How will our campaign serve our communities? Our families? **How will it resolve problems?** How will it alleviate suffering? In other words, how will it help people?

I believe we should THINK BIG and ACT SMALL. Instead of talking about changing the world, let's talk about changing a homeless person's life, a child's future, a family's health, or an industry's reputation. Instead of talking about changing the world, let's talk about changing . . .

a school without adequate supplies,
a student without money for college,
a disease without a cure,
an orphan without a family,
a slave without freedom.

Let's start by changing *one* thing at a time. *One* person at a time. I want you to dream big! But I also want you to live in the smallness of the day-to-day. By changing one life, one company, one mind, and one future, you can change the world.

You have three choices now that you've read this book. You can ignore it. You can apply it halfway (which is just as bad as ignoring it). Or you can take action. You can take steps. You can:

Own it.
Clarify it.
Plan it.
Do it.
Celebrate it.

And you can change the world. One campaign at a time.

THE END

ACKNOWLEDGEMENTS

Thank you to . . .

Jill Walker, for helping bring this project to completion.

Renee Weber, for working with me for the last 12 years and being a great friend and partner in crime.

Holly and Ben Crawshaw, who helped write, edit, and design the book. Without you, this project would not have happened at all. Not only are you great writers, editors, thinkers, and designers, but some of our family's best friends. Kacie and I love you guys, Lilah, and Buzz.

All the churches, nonprofits, and people who have hired us to help them with fundraising. Without you, this would not be possible.

Carey Nieuwhof, for allowing me to come up to Canada to run this book by you. For your help structuring the book and making it what it is. Also—let's go mountain bike riding again soon!

Louie, for always letting me throw ideas out to you, and for helping me decide on a winning cover.

And, finally, thank you to the Starbucks baristas (especially Zoe) who kept my coffee hot and flowing while I worked on this project.